*Planning for Success
in
Today's Changing Economy!*

Planning for Success
in
Today's Changing Economy!

You can't *save* your way to financial freedom!
Inflation & taxes will *eat you alive*!

Raymond Kallaher, Jr.

iUniverse, Inc.
New York   Bloomington   Shanghai

Planning for Success in Today's Changing Economy!
You can't *save* your way to financial freedom!
Inflation & taxes will *eat you alive*!

iUniverse books may be ordered through booksellers or by contacting:

iUniverse
1663 Liberty Drive
Bloomington, IN 47403
www.iuniverse.com
1-800-Authors (1-800-288-4677)

Because of the dynamic nature of the Internet, any Web addresses or links contained in this book may have changed since publication and may no longer be valid.

The information, ideas, and suggestions in this book are not intended to render professional advice. Before following any suggestions contained in this book, you should consult your personal accountant or other financial advisor. Neither the author nor the publisher shall be liable or responsible for any loss or damage allegedly arising as a consequence of your use or application of any information or suggestions in this book.

First Edition

ISBN: 978-0-595-50754-2 (pbk)
ISBN: 978-0-595-61636-7 (ebk)

Printed in the United States of America

This book is dedicated to my wonderful wife,
who has stood by me in good times and hard times.

TABLE OF CONTENTS

FOREWORD..xiii

INTRODUCTION... xv

PART ONE   SOME ECONOMIC FACTS 1

1   WHAT IS AN ECONOMY?...3

2   EVIDENCE OF THE CHANGING ECONOMY 5

3   U.S. HOUSEHOLD WEALTH AND INCOME............................8

4   INFLATION AND THE TIME VALUE OF MONEY 11

5   THE EFFECTS OF INFLATION AND TAXES ON INCOME 13

6   THE TRUTH ABOUT SAVINGS 16

7   THE COST OF HOME OWNERSHIP ... WHERE DO YOU
       WANT TO LIVE?...19

8   THE REAL ESTATE INVESTMENT GAME 22

9   THE TRUE COST OF OWNING AN AUTOMOBILE................24

10   RAISING BABY 26

11   EDUCATION...28

12   RETIREMENT 31

13   SOCIAL SECURITY AND MEDICARE 33

14   FUNDS REQUIRED FOR RETIREMENT 35

PART TWO   OPTIONS FOR SUCCESS...37

15   THE PSYCHOLOGY OF SUCCESS...................................39

16   EMERGING ECONOMIC OPPORTUNITY ... SOLVING
       THE TIME & MONEY PARADOX 42

17   THE TRUTH ABOUT TAXES 44

18   THE BUSINESS-TAX STRATEGY..47

19   STARTING A TRADITIONAL BUSINESS...................................49

20   A NEW VIEW OF MAKING MONEY 53

21   THE CONCEPT OF LEVERAGING...55

22   COMPENSATION..57

23   THE I-COMMMERCE CONCEPT..59

24   THE OPTIONS...64

BIBLIOGRAPHY..67

LIST OF ILLUSTRATIONS

List of Figures

Figure 1   Income Distribution in the U.S...8

Figure 2   Consumer Price Index and Inflation..12

Figure 3   Declining Value of the Dollar. 12

Figure 4   U.S. Worker Average Annual Raise..13

Figure 5   Long-term Effects of Inflation and Taxes. 15

Figure 6   Analysis of a Weekly Savings Program. 17

Figure 7   Effects of Inflation on $200 per Week Savings Plan...................18

Figure 8   Required Down Payment for Standard Home Loan. 21

Figure 9   Required Annual Income for Standard Home Loan....................21

Figure 10   Distribution of Education Levels, 2005.......................................29

Figure 11   Rising Cost of Education...29

Figure 12   Education and Occupation..30

Figure 13   Income Trajectory for a Typical Worker. 32

Figure 14   Individual/Employee vs. Business Tax Structure. 46

Figure 15   Individual vs. Business Income Statements. 46

Figure 16   Wealth Building Strategy. 48

Figure 17   Typical Allocation of the Distribution Dollar. 60

Figure 18   Internet Commerce Infrastructure...61

Figure 19   Integrated *I-Commerce* Business Model..63

List of Tables

Table 1   The Distribution of Wealth in the U.S. 9

Table 2   Yearly Impact of Inflation and Taxes on Annual Raise. 14

Table 3   Cost of Car Ownership. 24

Table 4   Cost Categories for Raising a Child. 26

Table 5   Projected Costs of Raising a Child Born in 2000
            through Age 17. 27

Table 6   Annual Income from Assets at Selected Return on
            Investments (ROI). 35

A Note from the Author

As I look back on my professional career I realize how fortunate I have been. I have had a challenging and exciting career, having contributed to some of the most high profile and scientifically advanced projects. I always had the opportunity and pleasure of working at the edge ... collaborating with many brilliant scientists and engineers as we pushed the technology envelope. I have worked for the best of companies and they have rewarded me well.

My personal life has also been blessed ... a marvelous ambitious wife, four wonderful and accomplished children, and two beautiful grandchildren (so far). However, as we were raising our family we experienced the effects of an ever-increasing cost of living that sometimes outpaced my salary growth. It was obvious that even an above average engineer's salary doesn't always provide adequate "after tax" cash flow with real growth that would enable us to build the dream lifestyle and financial success we wanted for our family.

Inflation and taxes were eating us alive! I was determined to find the answers. I did not realize that the *kind* of income mattered. There had to be a way for us to diversify and develop additional income—the right kind of income—without risking our hard earned financial resources and without jeopardizing the professional career that I enjoyed immensely.

I had spent my education and working career focused on science and engineering. Then, a few years ago, I realized that my understanding of economics, general business and finance was limited. The economy was changing but I didn't know how and why. I was determined to figure it out. I thus began an intensive study to gain a better understanding of the economy, how it works, and the ongoing changes due to globalization and the advancing Information Age. My research has led me to study the works of many recognized experts in these fields. I also have consulted numerous experts on the basic principles of leadership and success and how to apply them in the real world. This document captures an initial summary of this study.

We have put this knowledge and these principles to work with rewarding results. But, we are still learning and growing ... it's become a habit.

Ray Kallaher

FOREWORD

As society and the economy have become more complex over the past century, the ranks of professionals who help us with our money matters have grown:

- **The Financial Planner:** provides advice on asset allocation and long-term capital management, so as, hopefully, to maximize return on investment (ROI) and consequent financial security. *But we must first earn the money to acquire the assets to allocate!*

- **The Estate Planning Attorney:** assists in avoidance of Probate and to reduce inheritance taxes legitimately. *But we must first earn more than enough money that is not immediately needed, so we can acquire inheritable assets!*

- **The Real Estate Broker:** assists in the buying and selling of homes and investment in commercial properties. *But the buyer must first have the capital and income to afford the purchase or investment!*

- **The Mortgage Banker:** assists in providing the financing for real estate properties. *But the buyer must have the required down payment and the income to service the loan!*

- **The Life Insurance Agent:** offers policies that can provide necessary cash to protect one's survivors in case of untimely death of the primary breadwinner. *But we must first earn the discretionary income to pay the premiums!*

- **The Stock Broker:** advises us on what investments appear to give the best return related to a measure of risk. *But we must first earn the discretionary income to invest!*

- **The Accountant:** helps us manage our money, determine gross income and "adjusted gross income" through legitimate tax deductions, and helps work up our tax returns. *But we must first earn the gross income to "adjust"!*

Note that ALL of these traditional financial planning specialties require that we must **first have the money** to take advantage of them. It's a *Catch 22 ...* we must first have enough money to manage. The question is, how do we acquire enough money to make such management worthwhile?

It seems ironic that there are so many advisors and seminars on *how to* manage our assets, and on *how to* reduce our taxes, and on *how to* pass on our assets—but *so little* is devoted to the *all important initial questions*: 1) *"How do I earn enough money—**continuously**—to even need all these experts in money matters?* 2) *How do I earn enough money to acquire assets in the first place?* 3) *How do I improve my standard of living and maintain it through retirement?"*

To answer these questions, a new dynamic class of advisors has emerged. Often referred to as *Income Diversification Consultants*, they assist enterprising individuals in building financial independence by diversifying and developing multiple sources of income. Today, there is a growing market for those who have achieved extraordinary financial success to help others achieve the same.

> ***You can't <u>save</u> your way to financial independence!***
> ***You have to take a different path!***

INTRODUCTION

Are you really getting ahead financially?

One day Alice came to a fork in the road and saw a Cheshire cat in a tree.
"Which road do I take?" she asked.
His response was a question: "Where do you want to go?"
"I don't know," Alice answered.
"Then," said the cat, "it doesn't matter."
Lewis Carroll, THROUGH THE LOOKING GLASS, 1864

We all have a sincere desire for success. However, most people find it difficult to define what success actually means to them. Therefore, they let many wonderful opportunities pass by without even a look. Is it any wonder, therefore, that like Alice, when they come to a fork in their financial road, they don't know the best direction to take? In order to get anywhere financially, what is needed is a *roadmap* ... *a plan* that lays out **what we want, what we need to do, and a timetable of goals to get it**.

The dictionary defines *success* as: *the achievement of one's aim or goal*. In the 1970's Harvard University conducted a study that revealed the top 3-percent of highly successful people are those who took the time to prepare **written goals**. These top 3-percent achieved far more than the remaining 97-percent! In fact, these top 3-percent achieved twice as much as those who had goals but never wrote them down, and at least ten times more than the majority of those who didn't have goals at all. We can't let ourselves be fooled by the simplicity of this process. When we write down our goals, it helps our mind *tune-in* to achieve them.

Evidence shows that very few ever develop and follow through on their own personal plans to achieve financial success. Most rely on the *traditional financial plan*, whereby they are taught that if they get an education, get a safe secure job, work hard, and save money, they can be successful. But, the overwhelming evidence is that most people are struggling financially. The ever-increasing cost of living is pushing them into an insecure financial future. In today's economy, the experts advise that to build real financial security a job is not enough. However, for most, their job is probably their only plan. This plan is in the form of a job description that defines what an employee is hired to do. But it isn't the *employee's* plan ... it's the *employer's* plan for the employee. Also, the pay is based on what the job is worth, not what the individual is worth, and whatever raises the employee receives keeps pushing him or her into higher tax brackets. Alvin Toffler, in his epoch making book, *Future Shock*, advises that ... *"In today's economy, putting all of your eggs in the job basket may be the riskiest strategy of all."* A job provides no *leverage* against inflation and taxes. Financial success requires the vision and courage to follow a different path.

Most jobs provide neither the **money** nor the **time** to build a dream lifestyle. Financial experts advise individuals to diversify to develop multiple sources of income. Robert Kiyosaki, in his best selling book, *CASHFLOW Quadrant*, confirms that the kind of income matters. *Earned* income is a solo effort that requires one to show up and do work. *Passive* and *Portfolio* incomes are from *assets* and are on-going whether the individual is on the job or not. The smart strategy is to develop multiple on-going or *passive* cash flow streams with which to build enough cash reserves to acquire additional *income-producing* assets, thereby further expanding *passive* and *portfolio* income ... a wealth building cycle.

Life can only be understood *backward*; but it must be lived *forward*. Living forward involves traveling uncharted pathways. We can always look back with 20/20 hindsight. However, we are guided into the *uncertain* future only by our goals ... our plan. Success is not an end in itself ... it is a *journey* ... a *becoming* that is built on a **continuing succession of goals and achievement**. We must continually ask ourselves ... "Where do *I* want to be in 2 years, 5 years, 10 years?" ... and then plan accordingly. ***We deserve the financial success that we alone achieve!***

PART ONE

SOME ECONOMIC FACTS

1.0   WHAT IS AN ECONOMY?

An economy is a dynamic social environment in which people create and use resources to fulfill needs and desires. Today's economy has grown into a monument of complexity. Eric Beinhocker, in his brilliant book, *THE ORIGIN OF WEALTH, Evolution, Complexity, and the Radical Remaking of Economics,* writes that, "*The economy is something that most people take for granted in their daily lives and don't often think about. You are surrounded by economic activity and its results. Twenty four hours a day, seven days a week, the planet is abuzz with humans designing, organizing, manufacturing, servicing, transporting, communicating, buying and selling. The complexity of all this activity is mind-boggling.*"

As such, the experts have shown that an economy is a "bottom up" complex dynamical system in lieu of a "top down" control process. No government bureaucracy in the world has or will ever have the vision, the ability or the resources to "control" a vibrant dynamic economy! Innovation is NOT predictable. It is a convergence of enabling technologies into new economic activities that drive accommodating social changes.

As human ingenuity has driven economies to ever-increasing levels of complexity the means of economic activity and the respective social impacts have changed several times throughout human history.

The invention of tools and weapons launched the *Hunting-and-gathering economies,* which lasted more than 100,000 years. The discovery of farming and herding ushered in *agrarian economies*, which endured another 10,000 years. The labor and land intensive approach of these economies was succeeded by the machines and factories of the *industrial era.*

The *Industrial Age* (1760s–1960s) spawned the growth of the corporation and the concept of the *employee*. It also resulted in the growth of cities and the concentrated labor force, which supported the growth of mass production, labor unions, and the development of the banking system.

After almost 200 years, the industrial era gave way to the computers of the *information economy*. The first few decades of the *Information Age* used the computer as a number crunching tool, an industrial-style approach that used computers as "desktop factories" to perform routine brain work. Now, with the explosive takeoff of the *Internet*, we've entered the next phase of the information economy, which uses the computer less for data crunching and more for *connecting*: people to people, machine to machine, product to service, network to network, organization to organization, and all combinations thereof. This connectivity is totally changing the way the global economy functions … and these changes will be permanent.

The following decades will fulfill needs and desires by another set of arrangements. The Internet will be the driving force behind an entirely new economy characterized by connectivity, speed, and intangible value. One manifestation is that the economy is leaving behind the idea of stable solutions. Already, a successful business is neither at rest nor in focus at any given moment. The beginning, middle, and end of a product line and its distribution system are dissolving into each other as the ordinary and familiar step-by-step progression of research, design, production, distribution, payment, and consumption disappears.

The Industrial Age economy is gradually evolving into the *Internet-Commerce* economy, wherein consumers can connect directly with the producers. There are no longer boundaries between the consumer, the retailer, and the wholesaler. In this new *I-Economy* all of these functions are gradually, almost imperceptibly, being integrated into a new entity ... the *I-Commerce Business* ... that functions as wholesaler, retailer, and consumer all in one! Alvin Toffler, in his 1970 epoch-making book, *Future Shock*, termed this new concept *Prosumerism* ... the convergence of *production* and *consumption*.

2.0 EVIDENCE OF THE CHANGING ECONOMY

Tomorrow is happening today! Leading-edge enterprises like Microsoft, Google, Yahoo, Amazon.com, MySpace.com, and YouTube.com, are cashing in on the Internet and making fortunes for their key stakeholders, even after the dot.com bubble burst. Other highly successful Internet-based businesses are creating exciting revolutionary opportunities for enterprising individuals.

In their best selling book, *The Sovereign Individual*, economic forecasters James Davidson and Lord William Rees-Mogg predict that the twenty-first century will see the "death of jobs," as we know them. Only in recent years, they explain, has the word *job* come to imply permanent employment. Past generations understood the term to mean a one-time task that one was hired to do. A blacksmith, for instance, would get a job shoeing a horse. A seamstress would get a job sewing a dress. A carpenter would get a job building a house. But no one expected those jobs to be permanent. No one expected health benefits, pensions, or 401k's. Before the Industrial Age *permanent* employment was almost unknown.

The times they are a changin! In the Information Age, Rees-Mogg and Davidson predict, the word *job* will return to its older meaning. It will refer to specific and temporary tasks. Already, many major corporations are eliminating permanent job categories relying on temporary, or contract, workers for specific projects. Former Clinton Labor Secretary Robert Reich estimated in 1996 that 20 percent of the U.S. workforce is already self-employed.

Evidence shows that this trend is progressing. Many blue-collar jobs are becoming extinct. Information Age robots are replacing literally thousands of production line employees. Literally millions more manufacturing jobs are being exported to lower cost work forces in countries like China, India, Mexico, Indonesia, Thailand, Cambodia and the Philippines. Ford Motor Company is planning to eliminate over 75,000 jobs and close more than a dozen North American factories by 2012. GM is closing 14 plants and permanently eliminating 30,000 jobs in the U.S. and Canada. Chrysler recently announced that it is laying off an additional 15,000 workers. This trend isn't limited to the auto industry … it is across the entire economy from manufacturers to retailers. A review of the latest economic data shows that the manufacturing output as a percentage of U.S. Gross Domestic Product (GDP) has actually gone up over the last decade even as the number of workers in this sector of the economy has gone down. This is the result of Information Age *automation*.

Further evidence shows that this trend is not limited to blue-collar jobs. Experts predict that the U.S. will lose over **6 million** high-paid *white-collar* jobs to India in the next decade. Entire info-tech departments of many large companies are being *outsourced* to India, along with accounting services, healthcare services, banking and back office support. Many U.S. based software companies have made significant capital investments in software development facilities in India and actively outsource large portions of their new product development to highly skilled but lower cost Indian programmers. Management of these new product development activities along with integration and testing of the software modules into the complete final product is via the Internet ... on an international scale! Hewlett Packard and Dell operate major personal computer assembly plants in Bangalore, India's "Silicon Valley". This trend does not bode well for the future of the U.S. e-tech worker.

In his highly informative book, *CHINDIA, How China and India Are Revolutionizing Global Business*, Pete Engardio reveals that, "*China and India are transforming the global economy ... (they) are destined to become the chief drivers of global growth and will force immense adjustments on industries, societies, and economies in rich nations and poor.*" Note that China's largest information technology company, *Lenovo*, completed purchase of IBM's PC Division in 2005! IBM PCs now carry the *Made in China* label.

In other areas of the economy, the present U.S. mortgage and real estate crisis is impacting people in many ways. Thousands of workers in the banking and mortgage lending industry have lost their jobs. Mortgage and real estate related securities have lost millions of dollars in market value resulting in significant losses for investors. Home values are continuing on a downward trend resulting in significant and often complete loss of equity for homeowners. Many homeowners find themselves *upside down* with their mortgage. These people have high interest mortgages with principle balances above the appraised value of their homes, so they have no chance of refinancing. Unable to afford the adjusted high monthly payments their only option is foreclosure and destruction of their credit.

Obviously, "permanent" jobs will not disappear ... in fact, over time they will grow as the population grows. However, the nature of these jobs will change dramatically and competition for the best jobs will be fierce. These jobs will require higher levels of education and technical skills. The defining element of the emerging *Information Age* is the nature of the work performed. The emerging *Information Economy* places a premium on the generation and management of **knowledge**. The shift from the physical nature of *Industrial Age* jobs to the intangibility of information and knowledge in the *Information Age*, carries with it significant changes in occupations and industries. The change in the way work is organized and the nature of its output carries with it major social and economic change for workers and the places they work and live.

Everyone cannot live in the big city or close to work. The immense population would overwhelm the infrastructure and its supporting resources. Evidence of this is already with us in the form of gridlock and budget shortages of cities such as Los Angeles and New York, among others.

Recent economic forecasts predict that communities will undergo an evolution over the next 20 to 30 years. This evolution will witness an erosion of the distinction between cities and suburbs by creating more self-sustaining suburban communities. Cities and suburbs are going to change as they accommodate population growth. Advances in transportation and telecommunications technology will enable small, self-sufficient communities where people live closer to work or telecommute from home. Such *Information Age* communities will be more self-contained and environmentally sustainable over time.

These economic forecasts confirm the rise of *I-Commerce* and Internet sales as the costs of the traditional Industrial Age storefront business model continues to rise.

3.0   U.S. HOUSEHOLD WEALTH AND INCOME

Data from the U.S. Census Bureau was used to generate Figure 1, which shows the distribution of household gross income levels for the year 2005. Note that over 80-percent of U.S. households have annual incomes less than $100,000. Moreover, over 50-percent have annual incomes less than $50,000!

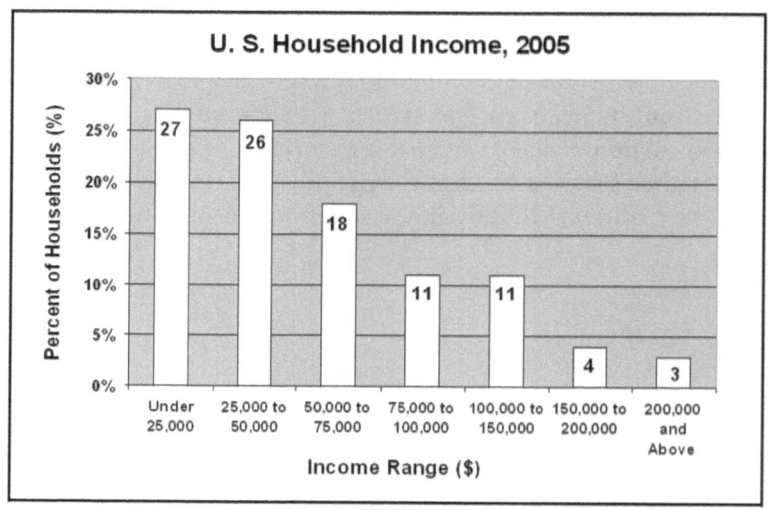

Figure 1. Income Distribution in the U.S.

Considering the ever-increasing cost of living, it's no wonder that the majority of households do not have the discretionary income to support an adequate savings and investment plan, much less a dream lifestyle.

As further evidence, Kevin Phillips, in his outstanding book *Wealth and Democracy, A Political History of the American Rich*, has documented the dramatic decline of disposable income of the U.S. worker. He documents that the disposable or discretionary income has been in steady decline since 1972, and this trend is predicted to continue. The data verifies, on the average, a decline of over **16%** over the past 30 years! **Inflation and taxes are eating U.S. middle class workers alive!** They're running out of money!

Kevin Phillips goes on to verify that only 10-percent of U.S. households control 90-percent of the wealth. Table 1 summarizes the categories of wealth. As seen, by every measure the top 10-percent on the average control 90-percent of the wealth: Business Assets (91.1%); Stocks (86.3%); Bonds (91.3%); Trusts (88%). Further review shows that the top 1-percent of U.S. households controls over 50-percent of the wealth!

Ownership of Corporate and Business Assets (1992)					
Segment	Business Assets	Stocks	Bonds	Trusts	Segment Average
Top 1%	61.6%	49.6%	62.4%	52.9%	56.6%
Next 9%	29.5%	36.7%	28.9%	35.1%	32.6%
Top 10%	91.1%	86.3%	91.3%	88.0%	89.2%
Everyone Else	8.9%	13.6%	8.7%	12.0%	10.8%
Source: Kevin Phillips, Wealth and Democracy, Broadway Books, 2002					

Table 1. The Distribution of Wealth in the U.S.

The definition of **rich**, according to some financial experts, is having a **net worth of at lease $5 Million and annual incomes in excess of $250,000**. In the U.S., this amounts to only 1 in 250,000 households, or only **0.0004-percent!** The *Forbes* business magazine has also ranked the four hundred richest Americans for 2006. "*It is now no longer enough to be just a multi-millionaire to appear on the list, you now have to be a billionaire to qualify. The group of 400 American billionaires increased their collective wealth by an impressive $120 billion, to have a total of $1.25 trillion US dollars!*" The rich are getting richer because the rich have more financial intelligence, meaning they are smarter when it comes to money matters than average folks!

History has shown that accumulations of great wealth have occurred during periods of great economic and social change. These changes are brought about by the emergence of new and revolutionary technologies. These emerging technologies, combined with new ways of doing business, have historically paved the way to new fortunes for the *paradigm pioneers* of the respective periods. Examples of the most recent revolutionary technologies are: the railroad, the telegraph, the telephone, radio and television, the airplane, the automobile, communication satellites, the computer, and the latest, the Internet. These technologies have driven economic and social changes that have required radical changes in thinking to adapt to and survive in the new world.

Kevin Phillips' research in *Wealth and Democracy*, confirms that, although the names of those in the top 10-percent have changed throughout history, the percentages and the 10-percent/90-percent ratio have so far remained remarkably constant. The latest emerging technologies of the Information Age, the computer and the Internet, have already created some of the largest fortunes in human history ... but the full impact of these new technologies is still to be felt in the marketplace. Information Age technology now permits the individual to connect directly with the economy. Experts predict that continuing growth of the emerging *I-Commerce Business paradigm* will result in a wider distribution of wealth.

4.0   INFLATION AND THE TIME VALUE OF MONEY

The *time value of money* is based on the idea that money available at the present time has more value than the same amount in the future, due to its earning power. This core principle of finance holds that, provided money can earn interest and a return on investment (ROI), any amount of money is worth more the sooner it is received. It is also referred to as the "present discount value" of money.

However, inflation can erode the value of money over time. There are basically two forms of inflation ... *monetary* inflation, and *price* inflation. *Monetary inflation* is basically the government, that is, the Federal Reserve, *cranking up the printing presses* and increasing the money supply, or *currency in circulation. Monetary inflation* is one **cause** of *price inflation*. When the government increases the money supply faster than the quantity of available goods and services in the marketplace increases, we have inflation ... a reduction in the value of the dollar or more dollars chasing fewer goods and services. It isn't that "greedy businesses" indiscriminately raise prices to make more money ... competition keeps this in check. *Causality* derives from the dollar being worth less because the supply of dollars has increased. Data shows that since 1960 the U.S. money supply has increased over **900-percent!** In response to this, businesses are forced to raise prices just to get the same value for their products.

The generally accepted measure of the value of money is the *Consumer Price Index (CPI)*. Figure 2 shows the CPI history from 1960 to 2000 ... it shows an increase of **375-percent!** Correspondingly, Figure 3 shows that over the same period of time, the dollar has lost nearly **90-percent** of its value! According to government statistics, this is reflected in an average annual inflation rate of **3.5-percent!** We may earn more money, but that money buys less in equivalent goods and services. So far, in today's competitive global economy the US dollar continues to lose its value ... against both the markets and other currencies around the world.

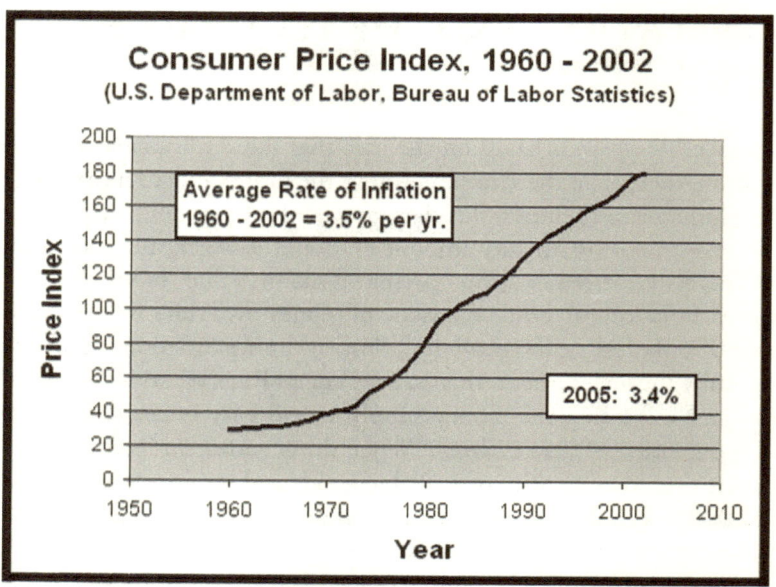

Figure 2. Consumer Price Index and Inflation.

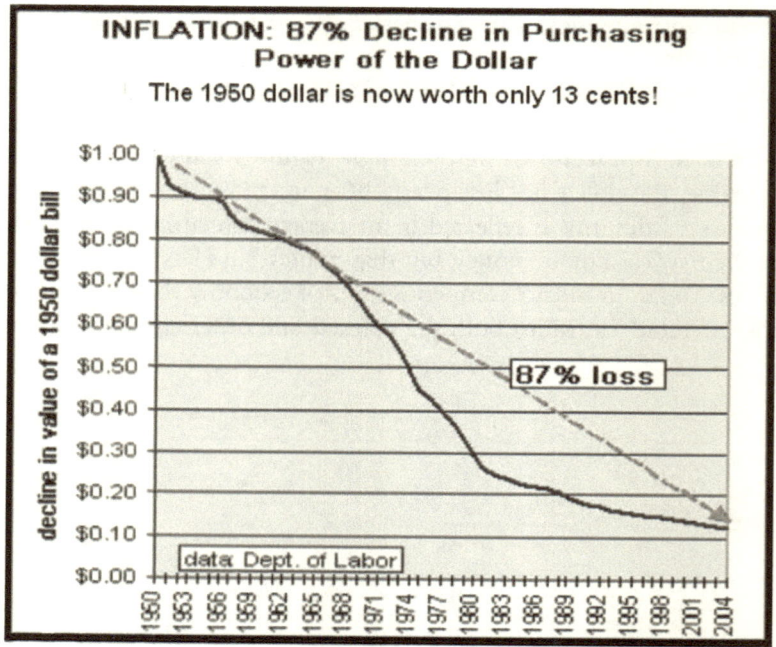

Figure 3. Declining Value of the Dollar.

5.0   THE EFFECTS OF INFLATION AND TAXES ON INCOME

U.S. workers are experiencing the disappearing raise! Millions of people today are working harder and harder and receive less and less in return for their efforts. The biggest expenses for the average U.S. worker are interest and taxes. Both put YOUR money into someone else's pocket. The interest paid on home mortgage, car loans, credit cards, and the like is income for someone else. Taxes go to support bloated government bureaucracies that hunger for more of your money … they never have enough! In other words, the typical middle-class employee or professional works to pay other people.

The U.S. Department of Labor, Dept. of Labor Statistics, has determined that the average annual rate of inflation since 1960 is about 3.5-percent, as seen in Figure 2. Also, over the same period of time, the Dept. of Labor Statistics indicate that the average annual wage and salary increase for the U.S. worker has been about 3.8-percent as shown in Figure 4. Simple calculations can illustrate the combined effect of inflation and taxes on annual wage and salary increase (Table 2). As can be seen, the impact of inflation and tax increase on an average annual 3.8-percent increase results in a **net loss** of around **1-percent** in purchasing power over a one-year period. With an above average 5-percent raise the worker breaks even.

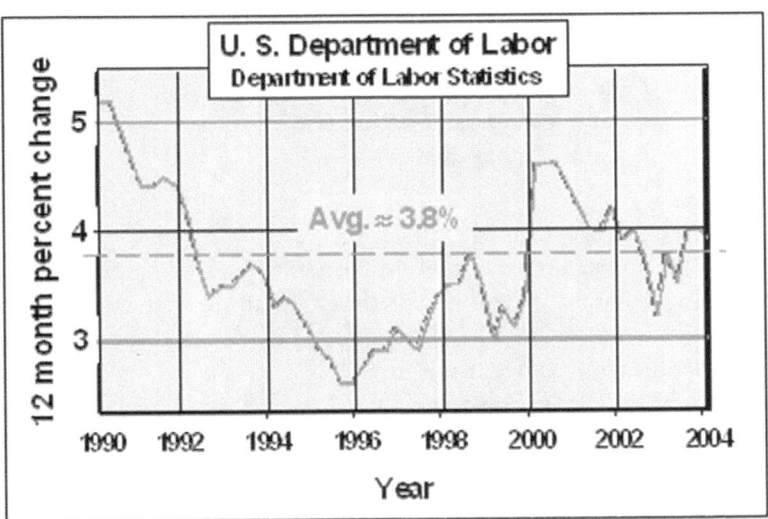

Figure 4. U.S. Worker Average Annual Raise.

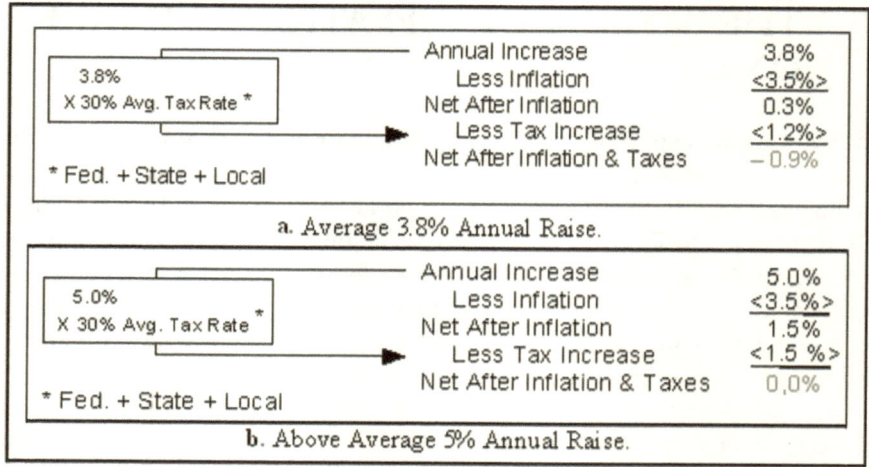

a. Average 3.8% Annual Raise.

b. Above Average 5% Annual Raise.

Table 2. Yearly Impact of Inflation and Taxes on Annual Raise.

The long-term effects can be seen in the curves of Figure 5. These curves are calculated using a very simple equation, which predicts income growth over time while taking into account the effects of taxes and inflation,

$$EffectiveNewSallary = StartingSallary \left\{ 1 + \left[r(1-t) - i \right] \right\}^{n} \quad \text{Equation 1}$$

where, r = average annual raise (%)
           t = average income tax rate (%)
           i = average annual inflation rate (%)
           n = number of years

Note that the average 3.8-percent raise (curve 1: $r = 3.5\%$, $t = 30\%$, $i = 3.5\%$) results in the continual, almost imperceptible loss of purchasing power and, therefore, decreasing standard of living over time. An above average 5-percent raise (curve 2: $r = 5\%$, $t = 30\%$, $i = 3.5\%$) just offsets inflation and the tax increases ... the worker just breaks even over time.

Things can be deceiving, however. Curve 3 represents the *paycheck dollars*, that is, the net after taxes income for a 5-percent raise without taking inflation into account (curve 3: $r = 5\%$, $t = 30\%$, $i = 0\%$) The worker can be misled into believing he or she is getting ahead by receiving more dollars in the paycheck, when actually they have to pay more taxes and the money that's left buys less in equivalent goods and services.

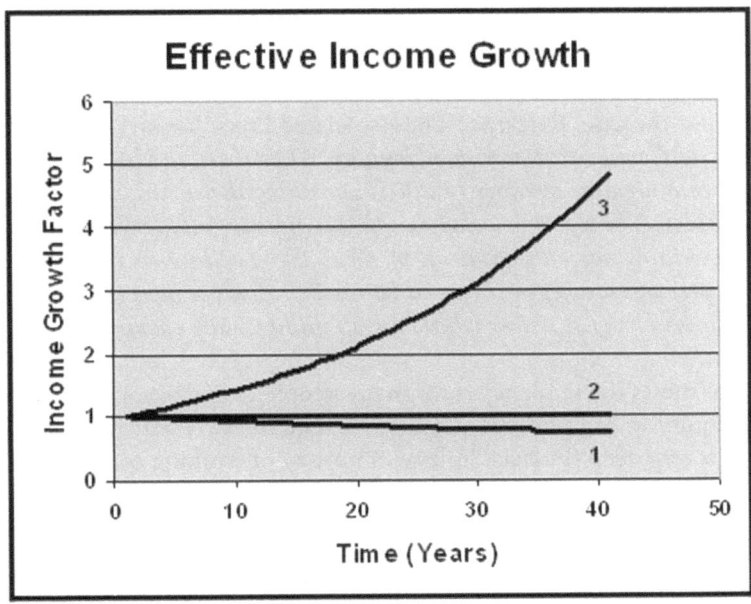

Figure 5. Long-term Effects of Inflation and Taxes.

6.0   THE TRUTH ABOUT SAVINGS

Everyone should have a disciplined savings program. However, evidence shows that this is not the case. Reference The Associated Press, January 2006: "*The U.S. Department of Commerce reported in January 2006 that the U.S. personal savings rate dipped into negative territory in 2005, something that hasn't happened since the Great Depression. The report revealed that the savings rate fell to **minus 0.5%**, meaning that Americans not only spent all of their after-tax income in 2005, but also dipped into previous savings or increased borrowing. Analysts have cautioned that this behavior was very risky at a time when over 80 million baby boomers are on the verge of retirement.*"

Evidence shows the tendency is for many people to live beyond their means by using the equity in their homes as an ATM. The result is that many are digging themselves a very deep financial hole with no way of working out of it!

The problem can be found in the conventional theory, which is to get a good education, get a safe secure job, live below our means and save money. It assumes that the worker will earn a sufficient income to have adequate discretionary funds, *after* covering living costs, to support a personal savings and investment program. Saving enough money isn't as easy as it sounds ...

- For many U.S. workers there aren't enough discretionary funds to save.
- Inflation and taxes erode the future value of whatever savings.

Figure 6 shows the requirements for a savings and investment program. It shows the growth of the *future value* of *weekly contributions* into an investment program for an average 10% compounded annual rate of return for "n" years. The curves were calculated using Equation 2, the equation for the growth of a continuous string of investments over time at a given return on investment (ROI). For example, a $2Million retirement account, even at **10-percent ROI,** takes over **30 years** for a $200 **weekly** investment, **26 years** for a $300 **weekly** investment, and **22 years** for a $500 **weekly** investment.

Financial advisors recommend that the individual should "save" 10-percent to 15-percent of their gross income per year. Using 15-percent, the income level to support the respective weekly savings can be calculated as follows:

- $200 per week savings requires $70,000 per year income
- $300 per week savings requires $104,000 per year income
- $500 per week savings requires $170,000 per year income

Those who have the income and discipline can eventually build a retirement fund. However, the effects of inflation need to be considered. Inflation is in effect a hidden tax … it will significantly reduce the future purchasing power of whatever savings we are fortunate to accumulate. Consider the $200 per week savings plan. The erosive effects of inflation can be illustrated in Figure 7. Here again, Equation 2 is used wherein the savings interest rate (i = 10%), or ROI, is reduced by the average inflation rate (3.5%) resulting in an effective ROI of i_E = 10% - 3.5% = 6.5%. As can be seen, inflation gradually erodes the future purchasing power of the nest egg over time … as much as **50-percent over 30 years!**

$$FutureValue = P(1+i)^n + \left[\frac{p(1+i)(1+i)^n - 1}{i} \right]$$ Equation 2

where, P = starting principle ($)
p = periodic investment ($)
i = average rate of return (interest %)
n = time (year)

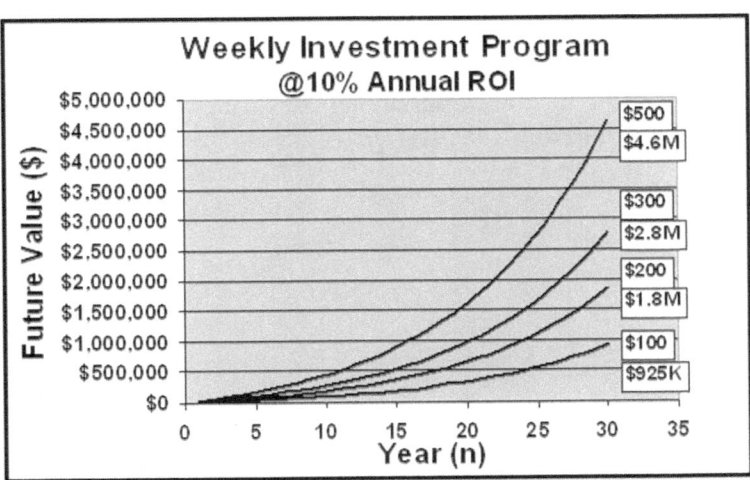

Figure 6. Analysis of a Weekly Savings Program.

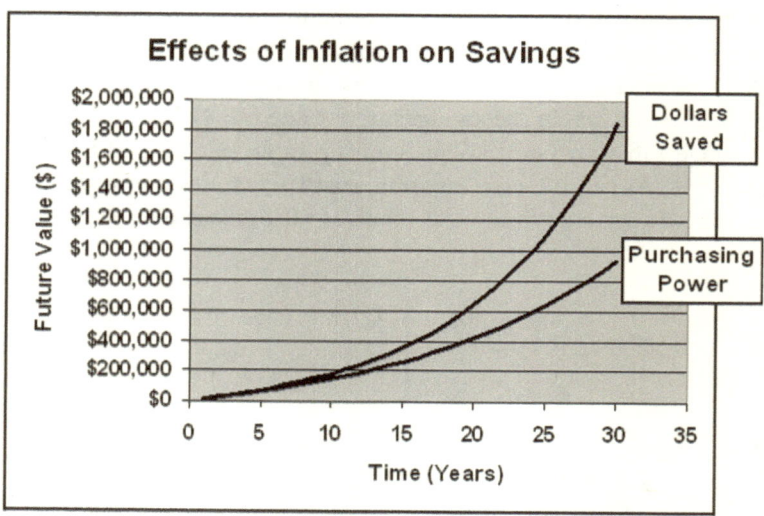

Figure 7. Effects of Inflation on $200 per Week Savings Plan.

This analysis shows that it takes **many years** of disciplined savings to build a retirement account. And during this time the worker still has to show up for work and pay the bills while sustaining the savings. The analysis confirms that ... it is nearly impossible for average workers to *save* their way to financial independence!

7.0   THE COST OF HOME OWNERSHIP …
WHERE DO YOU *WANT* TO LIVE?

A home is most likely the biggest expenditure an individual or family will make in their lifetime. For most people, it is their dream to "own" their own home. However, a home is very costly to acquire and maintain. The question is … is a home an *asset* or a *liability*?

Let's look at home ownership from purely an investment point of view. First, a home does not generate any income, that is, a home does not generate *positive cash flow*. ALL of the cash flow, in the form of mortgage payments, taxes and maintenance, is **negative**, which means it is out of the owner's pocket into other people's pockets. The "owner" can build equity over time, but the amount of equity depends on the state of the economy and the real estate market. Moreover, that equity is just on paper. In order to access this equity they either have to sell, refinance and take out cash, or get a home equity loan … in other words go further into debt.

In the real estate and mortgage crises of 1997 and 2006, many people discovered that they were "upside down" on their mortgage, meaning that the appraised value of their property was less than the principle of their mortgage. They could not refinance, yet they were still contractually liable for the mortgage payments!

In essence, therefore, a home *per se* is not the owner's asset … the owner's asset is a "paper asset" that is the *theoretical* equity in the home. In contractual terms the property is *primarily* the lender's asset as collateral against the loan! The lender is, in essence, making an investment in the borrower, and he fully expects to be repaid and make a profit in the form of interest paid. Note also that the income tax mortgage interest deduction amounts to no more than about 30-cents on the dollar … the remaining 70-cents is "out of pocket". Moreover, most people live in a home for just a few years and then move. They thereby assume a new mortgage, most often with added costs, which also shifts the mortgage payment period further out in time.

In other words, most people work all their lives paying for homes they may never truly own! Therefore, experts agree that a home should be looked upon as just that … home … a place to live and raise our families … not as an investment.

The 2006 real estate crisis has hit the banking and mortgage industry hard and has taught some institutions a hard-earned lesson. In response, lenders have "raised the bar" to cover their risk by tightening the requirements to obtain a mortgage. The days of "no down payment" loans are over! The financial aspects of an **owner-occupied** home purchase and mortgage payments can be analyzed as follows:

There are two primary requirements: 1) Adequate down payment, 2) Adequate income to service the loan.

- The required down payment for a loan is 20% **minimum.**
- The *debt ratio*, or [principle & interest (P&I) + taxes] divided by gross income, is 35% **maximum.**

For example, let's use these factors on a $500,000 home.

- Down payment = $500,000 x 0.20 = $100,000
- Amount to be financed = $400,000
  - o Assuming a 30 year fixed loan at 6%, the monthly P&I payments = $2,400
- Property taxes, based on $500,000 purchase price are estimated to be about $600 per month.
- Total monthly payments (P&I + Taxes) = $3,000
  - o Required **monthly** gross income for a debt ratio of 35% = $3,000 ÷ 0.35 = $8,570
  - o Required **annual** gross income = $8,570 x 12 months = **$102,840!**

The first problem is acquiring the $100,000 down payment. The second problem is having a **verifiable** income of over $100,000! The median home price in California as of January 2008 was $402,000 ... this is for ALL of California. The prices for even modest homes in the more desirable areas, like the CA coastal zone, still can exceed **$1 MILLION!** The same holds for other areas like New York, Boston, Chicago, et al. Whereas the home prices in some areas of the country are lower, so are the income levels.

Recall from above that over **80-percent** in the U.S. have incomes LESS than $100,000 per year and **50-percent** earn less than $50,000! It is easy to see that buying a dream home even in today's down market is a daunting task. Figures 8 and 9 show the required down payment and the required annual income respectively for home prices ranging from $250,000 to $1 Million. The calculations were made for a standard loan with 20-percent down payment and a 6-percent 30-year fixed loan at a 35-percent debt ratio ... detailed numbers will vary with the movement of interest rates and home values. A prospective homebuyer can use these curves to estimate affordability.

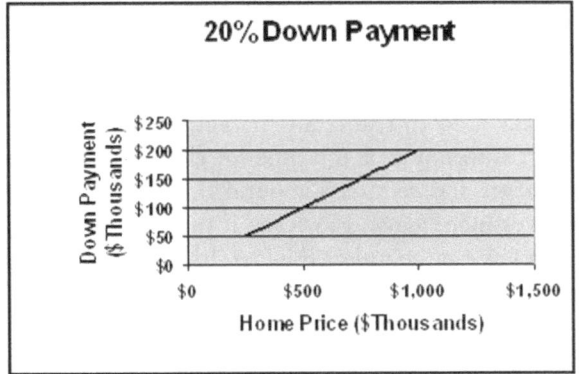

Figure 8. Required Down Payment for Standard Home Loan.

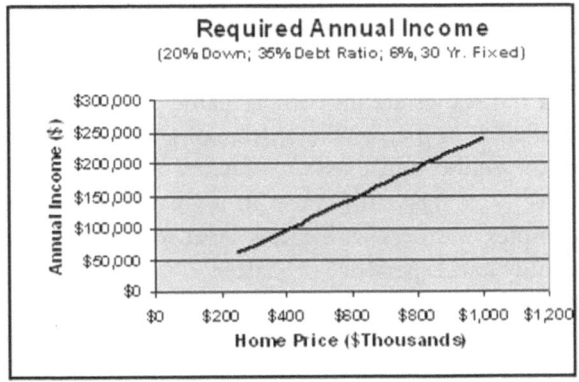

Figure 9. Required Annual Income for Standard Home Loan.

The historical trend in U.S. real estate prices over the past century is UP. The prices are leveraged by population growth, the increasing costs of land, materials, and labor, and of late, environmental regulations and community "slow growth" policies. Notwithstanding the temporary downward dip in real estate prices, due to the present real estate crisis, the probability is that home prices will soon recover and continue on their upward trend in the future.

8.0   THE REAL ESTATE INVESTMENT GAME

Real estate experts advise that today's real estate market is a "buyer's market". They site that in today's down real estate market, with declining property values and increasing foreclosures, now is the time for enterprising investors to reap the harvest. Advertisements and seminars abound that promise to reveal the secrets of the real estate investment game. However, it must be cautioned that real estate investment can be a risky game unless the investor has adequate cash reserves and a good understanding of the real estate market.

Real estate investment is a very serious game. The rules of real estate investment have changed dramatically. The days of zero down house flipping opportunities are over! Indeed, many of today's foreclosures are these zero down properties in which inexperienced investors have found themselves in a negative equity position and with inadequate cash reserves to ride out the market turn around. They not only loose their investment, they also have their credit ruined.

The majority of average folks do not have adequate cash reserves or the skills required to play in the real estate investment game. Much of their wealth is tied up in the equity of their home, which is decreasing in the declining market. To access this equity they either must sell or refinance and take out cash ... IF they have enough equity ... a very risky move in a volatile real estate market. Also, real estate is a complex business with many legal requirements and pitfalls that requires years of study and experience to master.

The financial arrangements for commercial investment properties are different from those of an owner-occupied purchase. First of all, for the average investor, most down payment requirements are on the order of 50-percent ... with a top credit rating, a friendly lender may come down to, maybe, 40-percent. Secondly, the interest rate for investment properties is higher, on the order of 2 to 3 points, than that for owner-occupied residential properties. Thirdly, in order to service the loan, either the investment must pencil out to a positive cash flow or be subsidized by the investor out of cash reserves. Finally, the investor must have verifiable sizeable personal income and additional assets to justify that he or she is worthy of the lender's risk.

Auctions of foreclosed properties are periodically held by lending institutions. If an investor wants to participate in a foreclosure auction, he or she must come with cashier checks in hand and pre-arranged financing ... the competition will include many *high-rollers* with enough capital to pay cash for the properties.

There are a number of excellent programs that teach the ins and outs of real estate investment. Some even provide support as the novice gains experience. However, the best of them are very expensive. Real estate can be a very profitable investment. But it is only for those investors with adequate risk capital and enough business savvy to manage the risks. The investor should not look for quick turn-around profits but should invest for the long term for positive cash flow and capital growth.

9.0   THE TRUE COST OF OWNING AN AUTOMOBILE

For some, an automobile can be as much a status symbol as it is a method of transportation. But for most people, an automobile is their second largest expenditure ... second only to their home. An automobile is an expensive item to buy and maintain and deserves detailed analysis to expose all of the hidden costs.

As an example, consider a luxury four-door sedan ... price tag, $64,000. A down payment of $6,000 leaves a net of $58,000 to be financed. A $58,000 loan at 6-percent interest for 7 years (84 months) requires monthly payments of $848. This calculates to be,

$$84 \text{ mo. X } \$848 = \$71,232 \text{ total payments}$$
$$\$71,232 - \$58,000 = \$13,232 \text{ total interest paid}$$

The total cost of ownership over the 7-year period can be calculated as follows (Table 3):

Interest cost		$13,232
Operating costs		
Insurance (7 x $500/yr)	$3,500	
Fuel (15,000 mi./yr. Avg.)	14,000	
Service (oil, tune-ups)	4,500	
Maintenance (tires, repairs)	4,800	
License tags	1,750	
Total		28,550
Depreciation [$64,000 – (10%/yr for 7 yr)]		33,000
Total cost of ownership		$74,782
$74,782 ÷ 7 years > $10,680 per year!		

Table 3. Cost of Car Ownership.

Paying **cash** for the car would save the interest cost and reduce the total cost to $61,550 or $8,800 per year. Leasing can reduce the monthly payments, but leasing comes with strict use limits along with its own hidden costs.

This is but one example. A broader analysis shows that, under similar arrangements of financing a car, the total annual cost of ownership can range from $7,500 for an economy car to over $25,000 for an ultra-luxury car. Certainly these costs will rise as the cost of oil and gasoline continue to escalate. The major factor in the escalation of gasoline prices is increasing worldwide demand for oil by other growing economies, primarily China and India, and the worldwide oil reserves are running out. Prices of $4.00 per gallon to even $5.00 per gallon in the U.S. have been predicted!

Combined commuting and other personal or recreational driving can easily average out to about 70 miles per day ... that's 25,550 miles per year. At $4.00 per gallon for a car with 30 miles per gallon mileage, it calculates out to be 852 gallons per year costing $3,408 per year or $284 per month. At $5.00 per gallon for the same car, the monthly gasoline cost increases to a whopping $4,260 per year or $355 per month! Add the other operating costs and the total cost of ownership is a sizeable portion of the family budget ... and this is for only one car. The average family has at least two cars, which increases the total operating costs to over **$560** per month at $4.00 per gallon and **$710** at $5.00 per gallon ... **plus** the monthly finance and depreciation costs! The costs of mobility are becoming a very large portion of the family budget.

In the meantime, an **employee** must cover the entire cost of ownership with *after-tax* dollars ... commuting and personal or recreational driving costs are NOT tax deductible. A **business owner**, however, can write off all business related auto expenses as *pre-tax* business expenses. Depending on the form of the business and the *mix* of personal vs. business driving, a sizeable portion of the cost of ownership can be accrued to the business.

10.0 RAISING BABY

In 2000 a U.S. Department of Agriculture report documented the cost of raising a child from birth to age 17. The report showed that in 1960 a middle-income family spent about $147,000 whereas a similar family spent about $166,000 for this purpose in 2000. Table 4 compares the respective cost categories for 1960 and 2000. Note that college costs are not included ... those are extra.

Expense Item	1960	2000	Change
Food	24%	18%	-6%
Housing	32%	33%	1%
Transportation	16%	15%	-1%
Child Care & Education	1%	10%	9%
Clothing	11%	6%	-5%
Health Care	4%	7%	3%
Miscelleneous	12%	11%	-1%
Total	100%	100%	0%

Table 4. Cost Categories for Raising a Child.

The report also estimated yearly and total accumulated future expenditures for children born in 2000 for low, middle, and high-income groups (Table 5). As can be seen, the total accumulated family expenses on a child through age 17 by the year 2017 are projected to be $171,460 for the lowest income group, $233,530 for those in the middle, and up to $340,130 for the highest. And these costs must be covered with **after-tax** dollars. Add the cost of college for each child and the total costs become quite sizeable ... and these costs for children born in later years are expected to rise. The little *bundles of joy* are not cheap.

Year	Age	Income Group		
		Lowest	Middle	Highest
2000	<1	$6,280	$8,740	$13,000
2001	1	6,520	9,070	13,490
2002	2	6,770	9,420	14,010
2003	3	7,180	10,040	14,850
2004	4	7,450	10,420	15,420
2005	5	7,740	10,820	16,000
2006	6	8,160	11,240	16,460
2007	7	8,470	11,679	17,090
2008	8	8,790	12,120	17,740
2009	9	9,130	12,520	18,210
2010	10	9,480	13,000	18,910
2011	11	9,840	13,490	19,620
2012	12	11,550	15,160	21,700
2013	13	11,980	15,740	11,520
2014	14	12,440	16,330	23,380
2015	15	12,740	17,250	24,950
2016	16	13,220	17,910	25,900
2017	17	13,720	18,590	26,880
Total		$171,460	$233,539	$329,130

Note: Estimates are for the younger child in husband-wife families with two children.

Table 5. Projected Costs of Raising a Child Born in 2000 through Age 17.

11.0 EDUCATION

The corporate world and the traditional business world in general, is a *credentialed* world. For most positions, many companies will not even talk to a candidate who doesn't have a college degree. The "union card" to the executive suite in most corporations is an MBA. It requires advanced technical degrees to open the door to senior positions in high-tech companies. Professions like medicine, dentistry and law require extensive and costly education beyond the basic four-year degree. Figure 10 shows the breakdown of the education levels in the U.S. for people over 25 for the year 2005.

On the average, college graduates earn twice as much as high school graduates. Clearly, one of the best investments we can make is in a college education ... for ourselves and for our children. College graduates hold an advantage over high school graduates in the labor market and the business world.

Corporate Professional Resource experts say that most *Information Age* jobs will require at least a Bachelor's degree, and the more senior positions will require advanced degrees. However, the data in Figure 10 shows that **over 70-percent** of U.S. workers do not have a full 4-year college degree, which will probably relegate most of them to lower paying dead-end service sector and manual labor jobs.

Data shows that college costs continue to escalate faster than the inflation rate. This can make paying for college or saving for a child's future college education a daunting task. According to *The College Board* and investment firm *Standard & Poor's*, the projected average cost for a newborn's four-year degree at a public college will total over $110,000, including tuition, books, room and board, and miscellaneous expenses. And this doesn't include *fun money*. This will require an **annual** savings of $4,200, assuming an average annual 5-percent interest rate, for **18 years** in order to have the needed funds at the start of the freshman year. For a private college, tack on an additional $175,000 to the savings goal, bringing the required annual savings to over $12,000! Figure 11 illustrates the rising cost of college education.

The accelerating cost of higher education comes at a time when the emerging *Information Age Knowledge Economy* places a premium on the generation, management and utilization of knowledge. Among the changes being experienced is the rise of research and development functions across the entire economy. There is, therefore, the respective growing importance of education and training to meet demands for workers able to contribute *value added* in a knowledge economy. This, of course, places a premium on higher education.

Society will experience the polarization of population into those able to obtain education and benefit from a knowledge economy, and those isolated from its benefits. Figure 12 shows the relationship between educational attainment and occupation, underscoring the demands of the *Information Economy* for more workers with higher education. The higher paying jobs are available only to those with higher education.

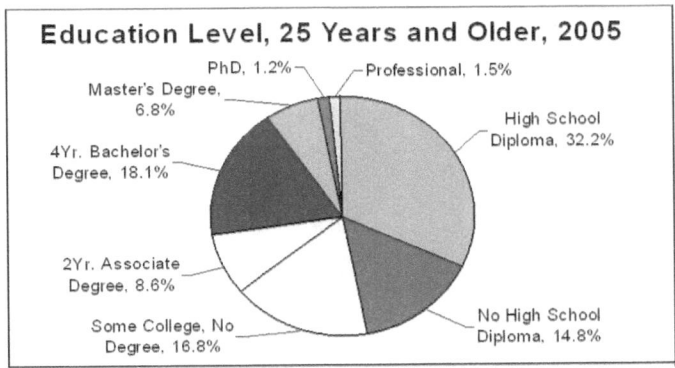

Figure 10. Distribution of Education Levels, 2005.

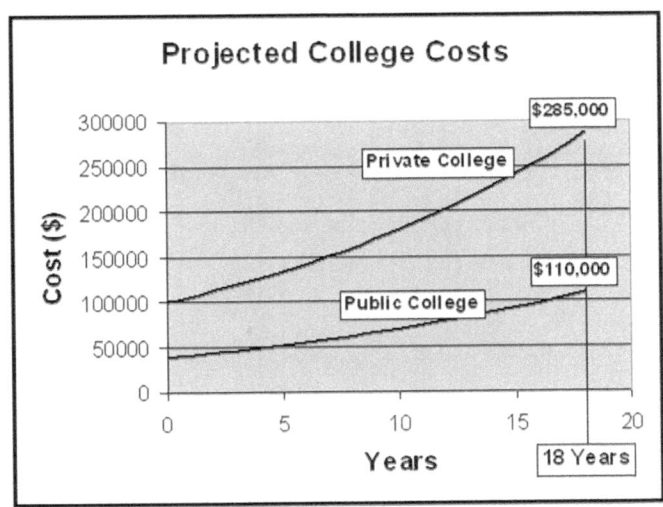

Figure 11. Rising Cost of Education.

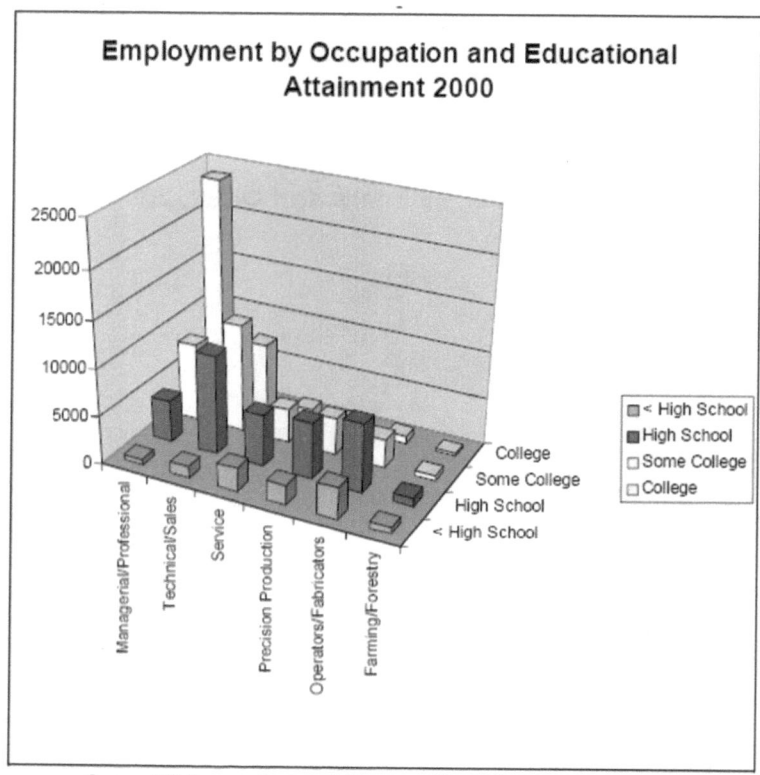

Source: US Census, Statistical Abstract of the United States 2001, Table 595

Figure 12. Education and Occupation.

12.0 RETIREMENT

Financial experts and government statistics show that 2 out of 3 U.S. workers are not prepared for retirement! Most think of retirement as something they do after completing 40 years on the job. Figure 13 illustrates the typical income trajectory, or pay curve, for an employee. The curve plots a typical normalized income growth factor over the working years. As an example, a $40,000 starting income would use the factor of 1.0 x $40,000 = $40,000 at year 1 for starting pay. This puts the new employee on one of a number of pay curves. Assuming advancement and expected raises over a working life, the worker may achieve in an income of 2.6 x $40,000 = $104,000 at year 40. This is an illustration of the corporate pay curves for an average employee. As shown, the raises in the early years are expected to be higher than those in the outlying years as the worker nears retirement.

All appears well and good as long as the worker is employed. Baring layoffs, and with good performance, most workers are able to stay just ahead of the rising cost of living. But this does not support a dream lifestyle or promise that the worker can retire in style. The problem arises when the worker retires. Under the usual circumstances the worker experiences a dramatic reduction in income. Retirement income usually derives from a mix of company pension, 401k, Social Security and other personal savings. Many financial advisors like to refer to this as being in a "lower tax bracket" ... INDEED! Most retirees are forced to make dramatic reductions in their cost of living and their lifestyle ... a very unpleasant alternative.

Planning for retirement must begin early and maintained throughout the working life. Since it isn't viewed as a high priority in the early years, retirement planning is often an afterthought. However, retirement comes faster than expected and can catch the retiree by surprise ... totally unprepared.

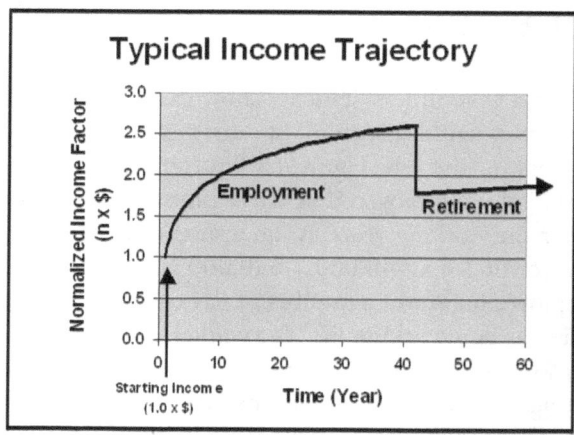

Figure 13. Income Trajectory for a Typical Worker.

Information Age opportunities offer a good solution. Through leveraging (to be discussed later) the individual can diversify and develop multiple income streams rather than relying on a single income from a job. These income streams then allow you to invest in additional *income-producing assets* that provide additional *permanent* cash flow. This permanent cash flow allows you to support your desired lifestyle, while not having to show up for work to earn a living. Building these assets fast enough allows you to retire in style at any age you plan for. Retirement is a matter of money, not age.

13.0 SOCIAL SECURITY AND MEDICARE

The 1930s brought the Great Depression, which led to the election of Franklin Delano Roosevelt as president. Roosevelt brought in Social Security in 1935, a solution to a problem we still have to solve today. In other words, the solution to a problem over 75 years ago has itself evolved into a bigger problem today. Other government programs that were meant to be solutions were Medicare (1955) and Medicaid (1966). Today, these problems are much bigger, and the future solutions will be costly and painful.

The first of more than 80 million baby boomers has just recently applied for Social Security. Every paycheck received by those 80 million baby boomers over the course of their working lives had a portion taken for the Social Security *trust fund*. The problem is that there is no money in the trust fund ... just government IOUs! It's primarily a pay-as-you-go system. Social Security payments to current recipients come from payments made into the system by today's workers and employers. In effect, **it's a giant government-run Ponzi scheme ... a government sponsored pyramid scheme!** Present estimates are that the government revenues allocated toward Social Security will run out by 2040, which means that there will not be enough workers paying into the system to meet the benefits expected by retirees.

Numerous previously appointed commissions have recommended combinations of benefit cuts and tax increases to reform Social Security. But congress and a series of presidents have ignored these recommendations while the baby-boom bubble keeps edging toward retirement age.

Medicare is in even bigger trouble than Social Security. Medicare's hospital insurance fund is predicted to run out of money in 2018. And yet, we witness unscrupulous politicians out-promising each other to expand benefits even further in order to buy votes!

None of us can stand the truth, and for good reason. Avoiding reality is a natural instinct and one of life's greatest pleasures. We all fantasize about getting rich. We all play the lottery. We all watch the "want to be a millionaire" game. And we all put off the trip to the dentist, doing our taxes, and making financial plans. The last thing we want is Uncle Sam telling us to save now to pay for a tidal wave of obligations coming when the baby boomers retire. So we make sure that doesn't happen. We hire politicians who tell us what we want to hear. They also dig us a deeper hole from which to emerge. The pending economic trauma of millions of retirees being driven into poverty is likely to overwhelm our society.

The eventual solution is going to be painful ... everyone is going to pay! ALL of the experts advise that individuals take immediate action to secure their own retirement. We cannot rely on Social Security and Medicare being there! And savings from a single source of income will not likely be enough.

14.0 FUNDS REQUIRED FOR RETIREMENT

FACT: Retirement is a function of money, not age! Upon retiring, people notice that the income from their job stops! Income in retirement over and above Social Security will depend on the amount of *income producing assets* the retiree has been able to acquire, including savings, real estate, stocks and bonds, and company pension. Table 6 lays out the amount of assets required to produce a desired income based on a defined rate of return. For example, a desired annual income of $100,000 requires $2 million in *income-producing* assets at a rate of return of 5-percent. The same $100,000 income at 10-percent ROI requires only $1 Million in assets.

Anyone who is relying on the equity in their home as a retirement asset just isn't facing reality. Home equity is essentially a non-liquid *theoretical number* that varies along with real estate market dynamics. This equity is accessible only upon sale of the home or if used as collateral for a second mortgage or home equity line of credit (HELOC) or to refinance and take out cash. The homeowner's options are to invest in another place to live or going further into debt. This is, in effect, kicking the real problem down the road … the real problem being lack of real assets!

Real assets—consisting of stocks, bonds, real estate (other than residence), and businesses—produce income. And this income continues for the life of the assets, not the life of the individual. The problem is three-fold: what assets do we want, how to acquire them, and how fast do we plan to acquire them. This requires careful planning and a *cash flow vehicle* to support the plan, particularly in the beginning phases of the plan. Discretionary income from a job alone is usually inadequate to support an accelerated wealth-building plan … additional sources of income will be required.

Assets ROI	5%	8%	10%
$2,500,000	$125,000	$200,000	$250,000
$2,000,000	$100,000	$160,000	$200,000
$1,500,000	$75,000	$120,000	$150,000
$1,000,000	$50,000	$80,000	$100,000
$500,000	$25,000	$40,000	$50,000

Table 6. Annual Income from Assets at Selected Return on Investments (ROI).

Pension plans are becoming rare in *corporate America*. Data shows that there are roughly 30,000 defined benefit pensions plans still in existence in 2008 out of over 100,000 about two decades ago. Also, if the worker is fortunate to have a traditional pension plan there is a chance that it may not be there in the years ahead as companies continue to eliminate them. Government data shows that the U.S. corporate pension system is **under funded** by an estimated **$400Billion!**

The U.S. Employee Benefit Research Institute recently released the results of a study on retirement age workers. The data shows that the number of workers age 65–69 continuing to work full time has significantly **increased from 36.4-percent in 1987 to 48.9-percent in 2005.** This is an increase of over 34-percent! And the number continues to climb. Recent surveys have derived the following statistics that confirm this trend:

- **75-percent** of Americans ages 45 and older say they don't have a financial plan.

- **63-percent** expect to work past age 65, most because of their financial situation.

- **74-percent** of Americans are worried they won't be able to maintain their standard of living in retirement.

- **66-percent** of Americans are concerned about outliving their money.

This data confirms the primary reason Americans are delaying retirement is that they can't afford to retire. The rising cost of living is outpacing the fixed income they would receive in retirement. Also, people are living longer and the relative inactivity of retirement isn't very appealing. A financially secure and productive retirement requires careful planning, and this planning must start early and be consistent throughout the working life.

PART TWO

OPTIONS FOR SUCCESS

15.0   THE PSYCHOLOGY OF SUCCESS

Success can happen only when people take the risk and move to action. First and foremost, however, a DREAM of success must take root. This dream can be inspired by the example of someone we admire and respect, or out of love for those who are special in our lives ... or it can result from self-motivation emanating from who we are.

Each of us is unique ... with our own unique personality ... our own character and appearance. But, have you ever been challenged by the intimidating question ... "*Just who do you think you are?*" If we think about it ... confrontation aside ... it's a very honest question ... a question that we should take very seriously.

The quest for success is a journey of discovery ... about ourselves and the world around us. Although everyone desires to be financially successful, research has shown that many aren't willing to do the necessary things to become successful. They quote reason after reason, and excuse after excuse. It's called creative avoidance. That's why only 1-percent of the people control over 50-percent of the wealth!

In most cases it's not what we don't know that prevents us from success ... it's what we *know* that just isn't so that's our greatest obstacle. Put another way, an obstacle to success is the *illusion of knowledge*. Failure to succeed is as much about what we *are doing* as well as what we *are not doing*! As such, the path to success is as much about unlearning as it is about learning. It must be recognized that it's one's old ways of thinking that have gotten them where they are today.

Building wealth is a process that begins with personal development. We must learn how to think, work and behave in order to build wealth. Building wealth requires discipline, physical energy, motivation and a desire to be successful. In addition, we must make responsible decisions and take responsibility for our own actions. These skills and characteristics often need to be developed and encouraged before they are effective. This involves a program of personal development.

Personal development involves more than learning a set of skills ... it is the process of developing natural strengths and overcoming weaknesses. Through personal development, we learn to increase our performance and minimize our risk. We also learn to manage our time and our finances more effectively, as well as developing our own potential. Through personal development, we become successful in all areas of our life.

Most believe that they live their lives based on choice. For the most part, however, we're like robots, running on automatic, ruled by our past conditioning and old habits. We are the products of our past programming ... a recording of information we have received and believed from the past, when we were too inexperienced to know any better. Our conditioning is not who we are or who we may want to be, but *who we have learned to be* from those around us ... most of whom are not financially successful.

Much of what shapes our beliefs comes from *other people's* beliefs. Regardless of their validity, beliefs are opinions that are passed around and around and then down from generation to generation to us. Those *other people* we associate with are very important. If we associate with successful people we develop habits for success ... if we associate with unsuccessful people we develop habits for failure.

Success is, first of all, an inside job. One of the reasons we don't achieve our dreams is that we desire to change our results without changing our thinking. Our lives today are the result of our thinking yesterday. Our life tomorrow will be determined by what we think today. Progress always requires change. Going to a higher level always requires a change in thinking.

Secondly, success is a team effort. A very vital component in the success equation is how many other people WE are willing to help become successful! Otherwise, what incentive do they have to help us? This requires developing leadership skills. Personal success without leadership ability brings only limited effectiveness. Leadership ability is always the lid on personal and organizational effectiveness.

Success is no accident. We won't just stumble upon it in the dark. Success is a skill ... a skill that can be learned by anyone, at any stage of the game. But we need a solid support system, a plan and, above all, *strong desire*. However, psychologists have proven that most people are risk averse and have a strong resistance to change. It is remarkable that so many people are willing to adjust to and actually justify literally miserable circumstances rather than risk their **ego** and do those things necessary to be different and take control of their circumstances. This is where the right support system steps in to provide motivation and direction.

Success is not an end in itself ... it is a process. Success also isn't transient ... it's a way of life! It derives from a *timetable* of a continuing succession of goals, action, and achievement fueled by a DREAM!

Whereas a goal without action is not achievable, there is no guarantee of success even with action. The degree of achievement is directly proportional to the degree of *persistent* action applied toward the goal backed by a program for personal growth. It also requires a willingness to risk failure, make adjustments and keep moving forward.

Successful people focus on *pleasing results*. Unsuccessful people focus on *pleasing methods*. Successful people are focused on the results they want to achieve. Unsuccessful people focus on liking what they have to do and accept whatever success that results. Successful people realize that achieving the desired results often requires doing unpleasant tasks ... *yet they do the tasks anyway.*

One of the most successful businessmen in U.S. history, Thomas J. Watson, the founder of *IBM Corporation*, always advised that ... *"The path to success is strewn with the stepping stones of failure."* Success without failure is unlikely. Without failure we don't gain experience and learn what to do next. We learn more from our failures than we do from our successes ... this is technically referred too as FEEDBACK.

Fear of failure is one of the greatest fears people have. Fear of failure is closely related to fear of criticism and fear of rejection. Successful people are risk takers who overcome their fear of failure. Fear freezes unsuccessful people in their circumstances. Unless we learn to embrace failure, we remain snugly tucked inside our *comfort zone.*

However, the degree of failure must be measured against *goals* ... without a goal there is no failure. That's why so many people hesitate to establish goals ... firm goals require commitment and action. Action, in turn, implies the process of *trial-and-error.* Yet many people are afraid to undertake the *trial* because they're too afraid of experiencing the *error.* They make the mistake of believing that all error is wrong and harmful, when actually it is both helpful and necessary.

This derives mostly from the influence of our education system. It is important to understand that getting a good education is vital for one's financial future. However, after many years of teacher influence along with many years of mid-term and final exams whereby grades are determined by the number of *right vs. wrong answers*, we tend to believe that we have to be *RIGHT* all the time ... the belief that we have to have all the answers before we make a move. This is all well and good in an academic environment but can be misleading in the real world where progress requires taking prudent risks ... the process of trial-and-error. Error provides the *feedback that points the way to success.* Only error pushes people to put together a new and better *trial*, leading through yet more errors and trials. This is the *learning process* by which we grow and through which we become who we need to BE to *justify* becoming successful.

In conclusion, consider this very important piece of wisdom. T. Harv Eker, a very successful and very, very rich man lectures to aspiring entrepreneurs based on his own personal experience. He writes in his inspiring book, *Secrets of the Millionaire Mind*, that ... *"I refer you to the Law of Income, which states, 'You will be paid in direct proportion to the value you deliver to the marketplace'."* He goes on to say that ... *"Life is not just about you. It's also about contributing to others. It's about living true to your mission and reason for being here on this earth at this time. It's about adding your piece of the puzzle to the world. Most people are so stuck in their egos that everything revolves around me, me, and more me. But if you want to be rich in the truest sense of the word, it can't only be about you. It has to include adding value to other people's lives."* This is profound advice from a very wise man!

16.0 EMERGING ECONOMIC OPPORTUNITY ... SOLVING THE TIME & MONEY PARADOX

Although massive global change is impacting the economic well being of many people, all is not doom and gloom. History has shown that the greatest opportunities present themselves during periods of technological and economic change. If current trends continue, many of today's massive corporate bureaucracies will soon dissolve into a galaxy of *Independent Business Owners (IBOs)*, connected by the Internet and fed through a network of supplier relationships. This will result in a wholesale transfer of wealth from corporate bureaucracies into the hands of rank-and-file *folks*. Rather than slaving away for the boss for a wage or salary, men and women of the twenty-first century will again work for themselves, earning an income commensurate with their efforts. The age of the pioneer will have returned.

We are seeing the role of the organization as a go-between diminish, as individuals have greater ability to participate directly in the larger sphere of economic activity and **reap the resulting financial harvest.** Success will arise from *networks* ... or as former Harvard Business School Professor Adam Brandenburger said, "*... economic webs, in which everyone is an active player creating and claiming value.*" The inevitable direction is toward the direct connection of the individual with the economy.

It used to be almost unavoidable in a product supply chain that a third-party distributor be in place, whose job was to break down truckloads of product from a manufacturer into smaller, multiple shipments to retailers. Thanks to greater *connectivity* and the drive to reduce costs and tangible assets by speeding up inventory dispersals, such physical distributorships are slowly disappearing. A customer can now connect directly with the producer via the Internet and the producer can ship directly to the customer.

What we are talking about is a reconceptualization of the individual as a node in a dynamic economic web. A node is a point of connection in a network to multiple other points. We used to think of companies staffed with employees, as being these nodes. Now, because of the pervasive connectivity, economic systems are now beginning to operate at a more granular level. Individuals are becoming the nodes, connected to one another and to the production segments of the economy via the Internet. The individual has the opportunity to operate as an independent business in the distribution of goods and services directly to the consumer. **HIGH-TECH joins with HIGH-TOUCH to maximize customer satisfaction and profits.**

The *Internet Commerce IBO* can operate from any vantage point, be it from home, while "vacationing" or lounging on the beach! There are numerous tax benefits! The marketplace is creating ways to compensate these *IBOs* ... and this compensation can be **substantial! The TIME and MONEY paradox has been solved!**

If history tells us one thing, it is that we should never underestimate the role that commerce plays in shaping society. The period of technological change we now live in ... dramatic and momentous though it may be ... is actually just the latest in a long line of similar developments that have shaped and molded societies throughout human history. Every once in a while, new technologies emerge and are applied in such a way that all aspects of society are affected, posing new challenges and offering immense opportunities for those paying attention ... the *paradigm pioneers*. The emerging Information Age ... the Information Economy ... is such a period.

We can run from the future but we cannot escape it ... and the future comes at us fast. **The evidence is overwhelming!** The economy is changing. There are exciting opportunities, but it is up to individuals to act ... the opportunities won't come to them. There has to be a sincere desire to change one's economic circumstances.

17.0 THE TRUTH ABOUT TAXES

IRS Code Section 162(a) states: *There shall be allowed as a deduction, all the ordinary and necessary expenses paid or incurred in the taxable year in carrying on any trade or business.*

Ordinary expenses:	Expenses that are normal, common, and accepted under the circumstances by the business community.
Necessary expenses:	Expenses that are appropriate and helpful.

The U.S. Supreme Court has upheld a taxpayer's right to, "*… decrease the amount of what otherwise would be taxes, or altogether avoid them, by means of which the law permits.*" [Helvering vs. Gregory, 293, U.S. 454 (1935)].

Everyone should rightfully pay their fair share of taxes to support the cost of our government operations. However, there are strong differences of opinion among the various quarters of our government as to what actually constitutes *fair share*. The wealthy, as a class, have a better understanding of these contrasting views than average taxpayers. They have always appreciated the different aspects of the tax laws as they apply to business in contrast to those that apply to the individual taxpayer. This has provided them a strategic advantage in the *financial success game*.

In 1943 Congress passed the *Current Tax Payment Act*. This Act implemented *tax withholding* whereby employers were now required to withhold income taxes from *employee* pay. Income tax withholding by States soon followed.

In 1986 Congress passed the *Tax Reform Act of 1986*. A major component of this Act was the implementation of strict limits on *tax shelters*, especially real estate investments.

Both of these Acts had major negative impacts on the U.S. economy at the time. However, they are but two of the many Tax Bills that the U.S. government has implemented over the years that have resulted in the gradual reduction or elimination of tax deductions for individuals. To this extent, average U.S. workers—employees and self-employed—continue to lose what little leverage against taxes they have left.

Even today, many "big government" advocates continue their efforts to close what they sarcastically refer to as *tax loopholes* … as if somebody is getting away with something unfair. In fact, taxpayers who take advantage of *loopholes* are actually working legally within the tax laws. As it is, even under present regulations, high-paid *employees* find that as their income grows they loose many deductions they previously had, such as home mortgage interest … it's called the *Alternative Minimum Tax (AMT)*. Also, some *anti-loophole advocates*, at both the federal and various state levels, are actually pursuing the elimination of the home mortgage interest deduction as if it is a *loophole* that is unfair to those who are not homeowners. If this ever happens we'll really see the bottom fall out of the real estate market! Whatever equity people have in their homes will disappear over night!

As an employee, your earnings are taxed and the taxes withheld even before you get your paycheck. The self-employed must make quarterly estimated income tax payments to the IRS. The sequence goes like this:

EARNED INCOME ⇒ TAXED ⇒ SPEND

If the income comes from or passes through a business, the sequence goes like this:

GROSS INCOME ⇒ SPEND ⇒ TAXED

With a business you can legally deduct business related "expenses" against the earnings before the government gets to it. This is shown schematically in Figure 14. The employee has the tax "withheld" before receiving the paycheck. However, a business has a DETOUR around the government in the form of business related expenses. As can be seen, taxes are against gross profit *after* expenses. The tax regulations favor business.

A comparison of typical personal and business income statements is provided in Figure 15. During the initial start-up phase of a business, the losses can be transferred to the IRS Form 1040, which reduce personal taxable income. Line 12 of the 1040 directs the taxpayer to IRS Form Schedule C, Income or Loss from Business.

The long-term objective is to grow a profitable business. However, examine the categories of business expenses. Ask yourself ... *which personal after-tax expenses are actually hidden potential business expenses?* When planned correctly, savings and investments can be made from within the business with *pre-tax* dollars. As Robert Kiyosaki points out in his book, *Loopholes of the Rich*, this is the wealth building strategy of the rich.

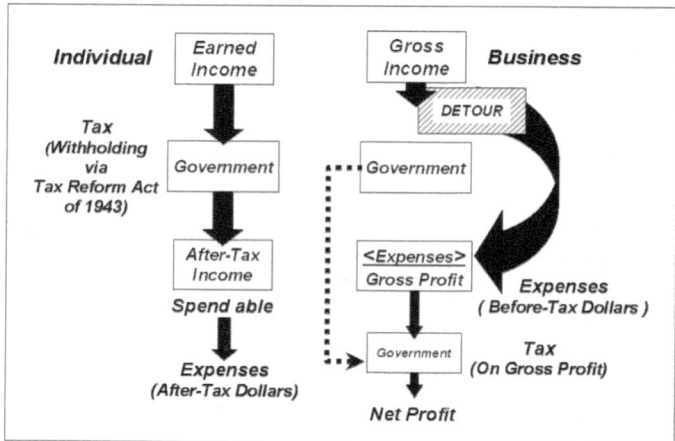

Figure 14. Individual/Employee vs. Business Tax Structure.

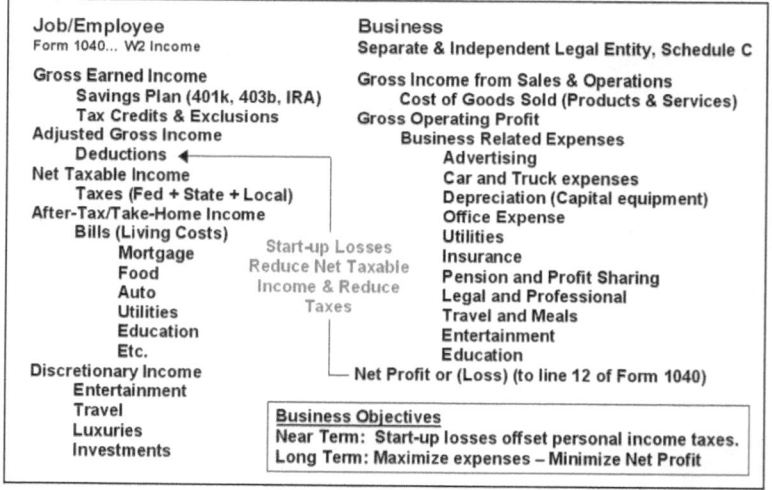

Figure 15. Individual vs. Business Income Statements.

18.0 THE BUSINESS-TAX STRATEGY

The new technologies of the Information Age offer unique opportunities for enterprising individuals who want to take control of their financial future. Unlike traditional businesses, which require considerable up front investment and full time effort, *I-Commerce* business models require only minimal up-front expenses for such things as, business building tools and education materials, along with a small annual cost for Internet web site registration. And these costs and expenses are tax deductible. The business can be operated on a part-time basis without interfering with one's present job or profession. This is the best of both worlds.

The first objective is to learn the ins and outs of running a profitable business … it's considerably different from being an employee. **You need a proven vehicle with which you can EARN while you are LEARNING at the same time.** The long-term strategy is to build a profitable business and build adequate cash reserves to eliminate debts and *invest in income-producing assets … **with pre-tax dollars**.* This is illustrated in Figure 16. This is a key benefit of owning a business. It is the legal way of building great wealth … by those who understand and operate within the IRS regulations.

First of all, the business cash flow comes with deductible operating expenses, which provide leverage against taxes. Secondly, there are self-adapting features of a business within the economy, such as the owner's access to products at wholesale that provide leverage against inflation. The individual can literally double, triple even quadruple total income or more—job income plus business income—while at the same time gaining valuable business experience. There is another very valuable compounding benefit in that the business experience, success principles and people skills learned through the business program make the employee more valuable to the employer.

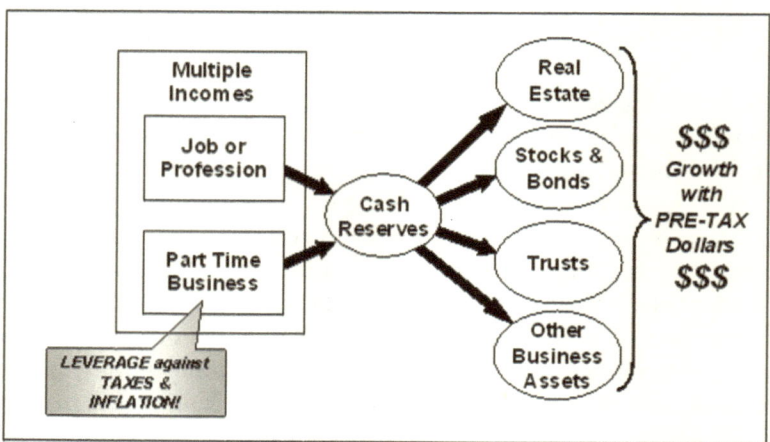

Figure 16. Wealth Building Strategy.

With simple planning and operation of the business in accordance with IRS regulations, the individual, as an *I-Commerce Independent Business Owner,* has the same tax advantages as any major company. The best of these *I-Commerce* programs offer education and professional support with personal mentoring, along with financial incentives—at no cost to you—for the mentors to help the new business owner to grow to full potential. It can be an exciting and rewarding journey for the right people.

19.0 STARTING A TRADITIONAL BUSINESS

The bookstores abound with numerous books written by successful experts on the glamour and on the hows of starting a business. However, few highlight the downside of starting and running a traditional business. Starting a traditional storefront or "brick and mortar" business in today's society and today's economy is a very complex and costly venture. Getting a business venture up and running takes business skills and personality traits that aren't all that common. Anyone who is contemplating starting their own business must consider the following questions very carefully:

- Do I have organizing ability, personal drive and leadership qualities?
- Do I know how to sell?
- Am I in good enough physical health to endure long hours?
- Am I psychologically ready to take risks?
- Am I prepared to wait several months before making a profit?
- Do I have specific expertise in the business I want to start?
- Do I know how to find my particular market niche and how to identify customers?
- Can I obtain adequate capital to cover start-up and operating costs?
- Do I thrive on thinking ahead and planning for the future?
- Am I willing to put forth the effort to make it happen?

Whether it's a franchise or your own unique business idea, the costs and risks of starting a traditional business are substantial. There are also numerous legal and administrative aspects that must be considered. Some specifics are as follows:

- Capital formation
  - o Starting a traditional business isn't cheap. Franchises cost $Hundreds of Thousands, even up to a $Million or more for those that have proven success. Even simple storefront businesses like clothing stores, gift shops, and the like can cost upwards to $250,000 to organize, plus another $200,000 to $300,000 or more for inventory.
  - o Securing adequate financing is a primary concern. Most people do not personally possess all the resources it takes to get a business up and running. The business owner will, however, have to invest his or her money to prove commitment to potential investors.

- o   When promoting to potential investors there are strict Federal and State regulations that must be followed. Failure to follow these regulations can result in prosecution and fines or imprisonment or both.

- o   Promotion of the business and sale of stock to prospective investors requires a good business plan ... and the founder needs good sales skills to promote the project.

- Licensing and permit processes
  - o   Most communities require a thorough environmental impact study, at the prospective owner's expense, and approval **before** initiating the business formation and start-up phase.

- Location and facilities
  - o   Location of the business depends on the type of business, whether retail, service or manufacturing ... prime locations can be very expensive.
  - o   The three options are: buy, build, lease
    - ✓ Buying existing facilities requires additional costly modifications, along with government approval, to accommodate the new business.
    - ✓ Building new facilities requires lengthy and costly design and construction, along with government approval.
    - ✓ Leasing involves finding adequate existing facilities and costly leasehold improvements to accommodate the business along with complex multiyear leasing agreements. The business owner is liable for lease payments even if the business fails.

- Capital equipment
  - o   Capital equipment costs depend on the type of business, whether retail, service or manufacturing
    - ✓ Manufacturing support equipment can be very costly, where as retail and service businesses tend to require less expensive fixtures and equipment.

- Legal
  - o   For tax and legal reasons, the owner must decide which form the business will take, whether a C-Corporation, Limited Liability Corporation (LLC), S-Corporation, Partnership, or Sole Proprietorship. Each form has its associated costs of formation and personal liability tradeoffs. There are also strict Federal and State regulations associated with each.

- o Filings with the respective governmental agencies must be accurate and thorough, and associated attorney's fees can be very costly.
- o Numerous complex Federal, State, and Local regulations that the business must follow, along with potential lawsuits (we are a very litigiously opportunistic society) dictate the need for continuing and expensive legal counsel.

- Employees
  - o Recruiting qualified employees to an unproven new business can be difficult. Recruiting organizations, whether captive or outside, can be very expensive.
  - o Start-up businesses tend to have a high turnover rate. Retaining employees takes promotion, benefits, training and opportunity for growth with the company.
    - ✓ Employee pay must be competitive with other businesses. Payroll must be properly managed and on time.
    - ✓ Medical and dental insurance along with retirement benefits are very costly. Retirement programs must also adhere to strict Federal and State regulations.
  - o Employees come with strict Federal, State and Local regulations. Failure to adhere to these regulations can result in prosecution and fines.
    - ✓ Federal: IRS and Social Security Administration regulations; anti-discrimination laws.
    - ✓ State: Income Tax regulations, rules governing hiring and firing, rules for the disabled,
    - ✓ Local: Local business taxes, environmental protection laws, etc.
- Other operating expenses add to the cost of doing business
  - o Advertisement
  - o Liability Insurance
  - o Office supplies
  - o Utilities
  - o Maintenance

As can be seen from the above, starting a traditional new business can be a very complex, very time consuming, and very costly exercise. And after all of this—the investment of money, time, efforts and emotions—the U.S. Small Business

Administration (SBA) statistics show that five out of ten new businesses fail within five years, and only one out of a hundred are still in existence after ten years.

20.0   A NEW VIEW OF MAKING MONEY

Strong advice from financial experts is to DIVERSIFY, DIVERSIFY, DIVERSY! Our education system focuses primarily on preparing us for the *job market* … to be an *employee* who works for someone else and collects a W-2 wage or salary. This is the traditional role of the education system … to prepare an educated labor force for industry and business … and our education system has been very successful in this role. However, students for the most part are *mentally and emotionally conditioned* for the job market. There is little opportunity to adequately treat the subject of *money, financial independence* and the concepts for *building wealth*. Students are led to believe that once they have a diploma or degree, their choice of good jobs will be waiting for them. However, the ebb and flow of the economy doesn't guarantee that enough good jobs will be available.

Professionals, such as doctors, dentists, lawyers, go through additional extensive and costly education and licensing processes in order to be *self-employed* … basically working for themselves. The professional is technically an owner-employee who is dedicated to the full-time practice of a profession … as such, the professional is the *primary or sole source* of a *single* income stream. If they're not personally treating patients or serving clients they don't make money.

Traditional small businesses, such as a franchise, an auto repair shop, plumbing or electrical contractor, gift shop, etc., have high buy-in and start-up costs and require full-time dedication by the owner to operate. Competition is also very fierce. Although the income can be above average it is nonetheless time limited … limited by available operating hours and the amount of time the *individual* can devote to personal operation of the business. Also, recall that SBA data documents that nine out of ten new small businesses fail in the first five years, and only one out of a hundred is still operating after ten years … **a 99-percent failure rate!** The Las Vegas gaming tables offer better odds.

Conventional theory assumes that the individual will have left-over money to save and invest in traditional instruments, such as stocks, bonds, mutual funds, real estate. These are traditional forms of investment that are *money-leveraging instruments* for which we must first have the discretionary money to invest.

Most employees and professionals enjoy their occupations … they invest considerable time, effort and money to get ahead. Many, however, fully realize that in today's changing economy, relying on a single source of income is a risky strategy. The single income may not net enough discretionary income after taxes and covering living costs to support an adequate investment program much less a dream lifestyle. Also, as many have experienced, their income can disappear over night due to circumstances beyond the their control with devastating consequences.

A fundamental principle of building wealth is **leveraging. Leveraging allows us to transcend time and money, and gets TIME and MONEY working for us!** J. Paul Getty, once the richest man in the world is quoted as having said, *"I would rather have one percent of the efforts of a hundred people than a hundred percent of just my own efforts."* Employees or professionals cannot leverage their efforts. If they're not personally putting in the hours, treating patients or serving clients then they don't make money. Few people have the time or energy to build wealth and financial independence on their own. Financial success is tied directly to teamwork and the amount of leverage one can bring to bear.

21.0 THE CONCEPT OF LEVERAGING

Leveraging is a process of multiplying resources to accelerate the accomplishment of objectives. It is a classical technique as old as humanity itself ... a natural method of human organization and collaboration. Evidence of the results of leveraging has been spread throughout history. The great pyramids of Egypt are a perfect example. The Pharaohs could never have built the pyramids alone ... it took the coordinated efforts of thousands of artisans and laborers to accomplish such great deeds. The existence of the pyramids to this day is a testimony to their skills and coordinated efforts.

Leveraging in any form involves other people. There are basically four methods of leveraging: other people's money (OPM), other people's time (OPT), other people's efforts (OPE), and other people's contacts (OPC). Any human enterprise great or small requires the intelligent application of all four methods. Robert Kiyosaki, a very successful real estate investor and lecturer on financial intelligence, teaches through his *Rich Dad* programs that ... "*The reason less than 5% of all Americans are rich is because only 5% know how to use the power of leverage.*"

We leverage through OPM when we finance real estate or sell stock to finance a new business. The *stockholders equity* in the balance sheet of a company's financial statement is essentially OPM. Typical of OPE and OPT leveraging is the Industrial Age *corporate pyramid* ... the corporate organization structure. Networking is the leveraging of OPC whereby we build a network of friends, contacts, associates, and advisors.

Following through on OPE and OPT more thoroughly, the corporation is an enormously successful creation having produced the very enabling technologies leading to the Information Age. It is a perfect example of the prudent use of all four methods of leveraging and has served society well. However, the corporation is a fairly rigid bureaucratic structure wherein authority and power flow from the top down. Within this structure, the executives at the top leverage their efforts through their *downline* managers. The managers then gain leverage by delegating tasks to their subordinates, thus multiplying their personal efforts. That's where the leveraging stops ... the subordinates are primarily individual performers who cannot leverage their time.

The employee occupies a well-defined position with well-defined responsibilities and well-defined compensation. The income level also flows from the top down with the big salaries and fat bonuses available only to the few "big guys" at the top. Advancement and income growth for the employee are slow, highly competitive and takes many years of dedication and networking.

With the advancing Information Age and the associated advancement of the *I-Economy*, many companies find that they are unable to keep pace in the new dynamic global economy. The "top down" authority and decision process of the Industrial Age corporation is often too slow to react to the fast pace of the *I-Economy* technologies and market demands. Also, many of these corporations have literally billions of dollars tied up in aging fixed assets and it takes many billions of dollars more of OPM and literally years of OPE and OPT to restructure. With increasing costs of doing business and rapidly changing markets, many are unable to respond fast enough to compete as more agile and more efficient smaller companies and marketing organizations emerge to capture the business. As such, in response to lost business and to reduce costs, they are reorganizing and eliminating literally hundreds of thousands of well paying jobs.

In the process of adapting to the *I-Economy* many of the old-line companies have lost billions of dollars. The airlines and the auto and steel industries are perfect examples ... mergers, layoffs and bankruptcies have been common. The lives of many U.S. workers and their families have been devastated, as they lost their jobs and didn't know which direction to take at this fork in their economic road.

The emerging Information Age offers unique opportunities to apply leveraging. The rapidly forming *economic web* of *Internet Commerce* is wide open to enterprising individuals who have a strong desire for financial independence. The individual has the opportunity to take full advantage of all four methods of leveraging which are not accessible as an employee. Within the company the employee cannot use OPE or OPT to build multiple sources of income. The employee is compensated with only one wage or salary ... a single income.

The Information Age *I-Commerce* business paradigm affords opportunities not possible through the Industrial Age paradigm. Through fair and equitable leveraging, income is based on *effort* and *leadership*, and is not defined by the individual's *position* in some traditional business pyramid organization structure. Fair and equitable leveraging offers the individual equal opportunity to earn sizeable *leadership bonuses* and to build *residual* income. Residual income is money that keeps coming in long after the respective work is completed. Once residual income streams are developed, they keep on flowing, even when taking time off to lie on the beach. Only through residual income can we gain **freedom** through continuing income without having to show up for work. This is not possible with a job!

Leveraging allows the individual to build multiple income streams. The resulting cash reserves can then be used to acquire other income producing assets. When planned properly, some assets can be acquired through the business with pre-tax dollars. This can be derived through the *I-Commerce* business model without interfering with one's primary occupation. This is the new view of making money ... this is **financial independence!**

22.0 COMPENSATION

Question: "How much income do you deserve?" When asked this question, most tend to address it from the perspective of a W-2 wage or salary. This is understandable since our education system focuses on preparing us for the job market. As an employee we tend to think in terms of the "workweek" and how much we are paid by the hour or the week. We all understand how many hours are in the workweek, but consider this question instead: "How many *dollars* are there in a week?"

We all expect to be well compensated for our efforts and contributions. Although many dedicated employees build successful careers, when looking up the chain of command they observe the enormous salaries and fat bonuses given to those at the top. They observe that rank and file employees are compensated with only a few dollars to tens of dollars per hour while others are in a position to be compensated with literally **hundreds** or even **thousands** of dollars per hour or more! This is the real world of corporate America.

Compensation for an employee, the self-employed professional or the traditional business owner is essentially limited to a 1:1 ratio in one form or another. For the employee, 1 hour of work yields 1 hour of pay. The location of a small business, a medical or legal practice, along with the number of hours available to personally treat patients, service clients or serve customers are essentially other forms of the 1:1 ratio that bounds the income potential for the professional or traditional business owner.

With leveraging, however, we are able to expand the limits of efforts, time, space, and even money. Leveraging is powerful because small, singular efforts in small amounts of time with small amounts of effort can generate big results over time … it accelerates the accomplishment of goals. This phenomenon, common to the scientific theory of Nonlinear Dynamics, is described technically as *strong sensitivity to initial conditions*. Just a small change in the initial conditions can drastically change the long-term behavior of a system. Recalling that an economy is a complex dynamical system, this phenomenon applies directly to economics. It also applies to personal finances as well.

Leveraging is a powerful technique, which in any form, as stated before, involves other people. With leverage, the earning ratio is expanded from 1:1 … to 10:1 … to 100:1 … to 1,000:1 … even 10,000:1 or more! This is literally impossible with a job or as a professional or with a traditional "brick-and-mortar" business.

The *I-Commerce* business model has a low cost of entry yet has a huge earning potential. It affords each and every member of the program the opportunity to leverage their time, efforts and contacts, along with other people's efforts (OPE), other people's time (OPT), and other people's contacts (OPC). It is an ideal business environment that offers equal opportunity and high earnings potential through leadership. If your looking for the secret to building wealth, this is it ... otherwise you're stuck with 1:1.

This leads us back to the question of ... *"How many dollars are there in a week?"* The answer is ... *With leveraging it is virtually unlimited, based on the individual's leadership ability, competitive spirit, dedication to personal growth and persistent effort.*

23.0 THE I-COMMMERCE CONCEPT

The advancing information and communication technologies that are driving the Information Age are enabling new and more cost effective ways of doing business. Many business organizations, including *Fortune 500* companies are restructuring to integrate the *I-Commerce* business model into their operations. This business model eliminates the middlemen and the intermediate distribution inventories, along with permitting significant reductions in advertising costs. These cost reductions can then be passed on to the *prosumer* as earnings or savings.

At no time in human history has the individual been able to personally participate more directly in the economy than in today's *I-Economy*. The *I-Commerce Business Model* is unique in its ability to permit the aspiring entrepreneur to develop a profitable business without risking large front-end capital investment and the necessity of devoting full time effort to the enterprise, as does the traditional "brick and mortar" business model. The average U.S. worker has neither the time nor the money to risk on a traditional business venture while at the same time holding down a full time job and taking care of a family. Also, most U.S. workers do not have the training, business skills and experience to launch and operate a business … capital risk does not permit lengthy *on-the-job-training*! The *I-Commerce business model* offers unparalleled opportunity and hope for the individual with big dreams!

The Information Age *I-Economy* marketplace has evolved very lucrative methods to compensate the independent *I-Commerce* business owner. Income is earned through the distribution of products to the marketplace. Members build business networks, which in effect is a web of captive markets, without territorial, geographical or time limitations. Products are distributed through *prosumer* members of the network directly from producers thereby eliminating the costly middlemen.

A lucrative and equitable multi-level compensation schedule, supported by participating companies, redirects shares of the *distribution dollars* into the pockets of the *IBO* based on the volume of business that flows through his or her captive market or network. As a combined retailer, wholesaler and broker, the *prosumer IBO* has the opportunity to share in over **60-percent** of the product distribution dollar, as shown in Figure 17. As a consumer, the *IBO* has access to top quality products at discount or wholesale prices.

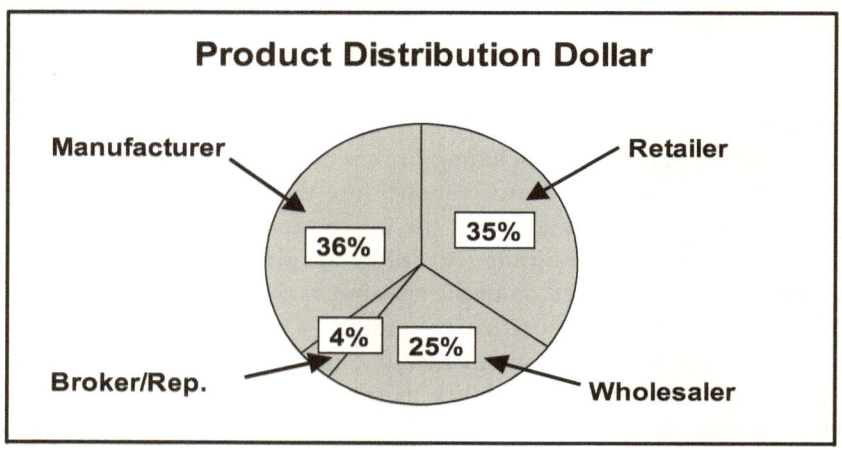

Figure 17. Typical Allocation of the Distribution Dollar.

U.S. Department of Commerce research estimates that the average household spends around $800 per month or $9,600 per year on household products, goods and services. Since there are about 120 MILLION U.S. households, this calculates out to be a **$1.2 TRILLION** annual market. This means that the *I-Commerce IBO* can compete for a share of the over 60-percent distribution portion of this market or over **$720 BILLION annually!** The *IBO* is free to build his or her captive market as big and as broad as desired. Income is limited only by competitive spirit and a willingness to grow and develop business and leadership skills.

Complete industries are captured in the *I-Commerce* equation. Figure 18 illustrates the wide variety of products, goods and services made available **at this time** through the *I-Commerce* infrastructure … emphasis on **at this time!** The *I-Economy* is a rapidly expanding wildly dynamic system. Experts conjecture that 90-percent of the new products available in the marketplace by the year 2050 haven't even been invented yet!

This is an ideal environment for *I-Commerce* to flourish. The *I-Commerce business model* is basically a unique marketing and distribution system. It can select which new innovative products to accommodate for distribution within its system. This means that the *IBO* can focus attention on the most profitable aspects of the business … marketing and distribution … in lieu of sweating over the complex and problematic aspects of new product development.

For the *IBO*, of course, this involves a program of personal growth and developing business leadership skills. Fortunately, with *I-Commerce*, the IBO has the luxury of learning while earning without large front-end capital investment … the luxury of on-the-job training while enjoying additional income.

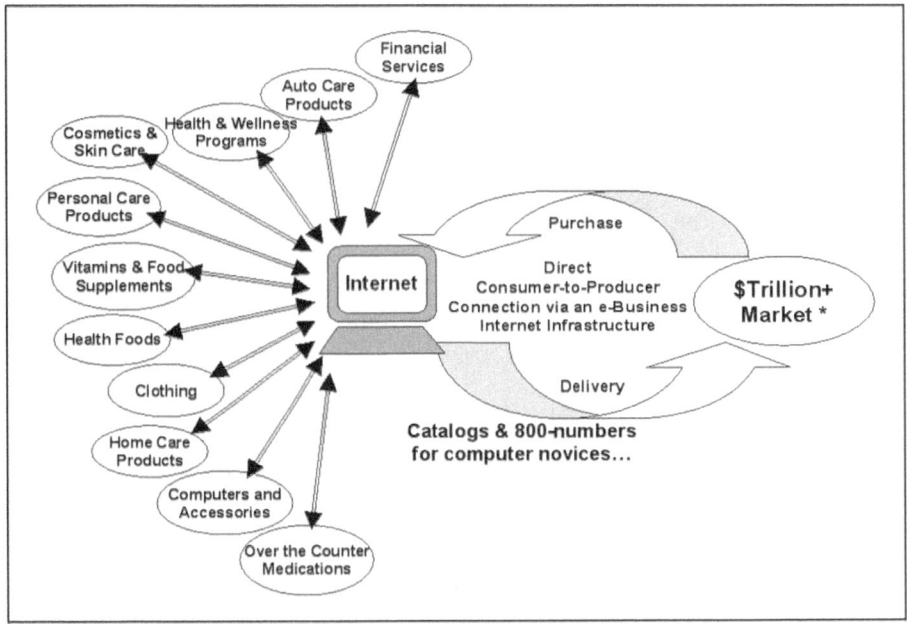

Figure 18. Internet Commerce Infrastructure.

As the Information Age advances, we are swept along by the flood of technical innovation. Mobilized to take the initiative, we are helping to accelerate the process, using and creating new and innovative ways to work and build wealth. At the heart of these innovations is the explosion of the new technologies of information and communication. These new technologies are about *connecting* … establishing and maintaining links, bridging distances, bringing people and businesses together in a vast *cybercommunity*.

And yet, as *I-Commerce* connects the whole world with high performance network infrastructure, and as this infrastructure establishes better links with friends, acquaintances and business associates, we psychologically tend to count on *the system* to facilitate communication, encourage innovation and the sharing of knowledge. In our quest to make our lives more efficient and reduce the amount of lost time, this new technical framework has exposed another problem. We have come to realize that we have missed the *social aspect* of the system as being as important as the technological aspect. Technology will only be efficient and facilitate communication if the *social foundation* of this connectivity advances along with the technology. As social beings, we need the human touch.

We have learned to freely communicate through voice mail and e-mail, and to "surf the web", but in so doing we have tended to distance human contact. While enjoying being captivated by these technologies, we tend to adapt more and more to the *high-tech* while missing *high-touch* ... personal association with other people. While voice mail, email and the Internet are becoming integrated into most of our lives, we must not allow high-tech communication to displace high-touch *commune*-ication.

When we add the *human factor* into the business equation, it changes everything. It brings in teamwork, support, motivation, trust and leadership. This *human factor* is the very heart and soul of the *I-Commerce* business network model. The continuing growth of *I-Commerce* and its acceptance in the *I-Economy* marketplace are testimony to its pioneers and to the opportunity it offers the enterprising individual.

Scores of TV and radio ads are espousing the benefits of working from home via a home-based business. These ads show smiling faces giving testimony to high incomes while working from the comfort of their home. This concept appears attractive on the surface and does have some advantages over commuting long distances to a job every day. Few people, however, want to be confined to home for long hours every day while dealing with the marketplace only via telephone or the Internet like a telemarketer.

What about a business model that you can literally operate out of your hip pocket at any time and in any place you choose either part time or full time ... a business that you can build at your own pace while integrating it into your normal daily life with the accompanying tax advantages and income generating power ... a business that you take along with you whether going to the supermarket, taking the kids to soccer or vacationing in exotic places? This is real freedom and the very features that the *I-Commerce* business model offers ... the business of YOU! YOU are the business, and the business is YOU ... a business without walls connected to the Internet ... the ultimate in operational freedom!

As shown in Figure 19, *I-Commerce* is a well-integrated business model consisting of an established technical and product support infrastructure along with a strong leadership and business development support environment. All legal and regulatory aspects of the business have been put in place. Both the technical and social factors are combined to form a business model tailored for the *Information Age*.

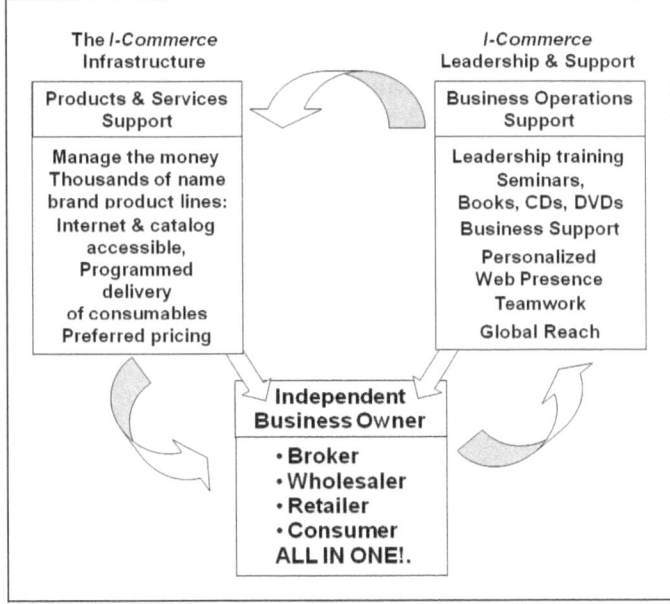

Figure 19. Integrated *I-Commerce* Business Model.

24.0 THE OPTIONS

The demands on our finances are **enormous**. Individuals cannot rely on the government or an employer to provide financial security ... it isn't their job. It's up to individuals to take control of their own financial future. Financial experts agree that this takes planning and a vehicle that provides alternative sources of income.

As the emerging Information Age and globalization continue to impact the financial well being of U.S. workers and their families, what options do they have? For those still employed what options do they have when realizing that the rising cost of living and increased taxes continue to outpace wage and salary increases? Here are the options:

- Go from job to job over a 40-year career looking for a "better" job.
    - You may make more money, but analysis shows that **inflation and taxes will eat you alive!**
    - Changing jobs too often or too soon damages credibility and reputation.
    - The era of abundant safe secure jobs is over.
- Get a second job.
    - This is only a short-term solution since people have only so much stamina.
    - Your primary employer may not permit it.
- Put the spouse to work.
    - There are diminishing returns due to the impact of income taxes. In the case of the wife, analysis shows that she may net only minimal additional income after paying for childcare.
    - This may expect too much and would detract from being the full-time parent that children deserve.
- Start a traditional small business.
    - The front-end investment and start-up costs are substantial.
    - Requires total full-time dedication.
    - S.B.A. statistics show that 9 out of 10 fail within 5 years, and only 1 out of 100 are still in existence after 10 years ... failure implies loss of invested capital.
- Wait for the government to solve your problems.

- o   This is the *Rip Van Winkle* solution ... you wake up older with the same problems.

- o   Government *solutions* always come with unforeseen consequences.

- o   Governments can only set policy ... history has shown that they are powerless to control the economy and the markets without devastating effects.

- •   Stay where you are ... "kick back" ... "wait and see what happens".

- o   You can "cut back" only so much ... pretty soon you're totally broke!

- o   By the time you decide to act it may be too late!

There is another exciting and very rewarding alternative. Numerous visionary organizations, including *Fortune 500* companies, are pioneering the *Information Age business paradigm*. Ambitious individuals can operate a profitable *I-Commerce* business, part time, without capital risk and without interfering with their primary occupation! The infrastructure and the education and support systems are already in place.

In his best selling book, *The BUSINESS SCHOOL*, Robert Kiyosaki states that ... "*The richest people in the world build networks. Everyone else is trained to look for work.*" And as the saying goes ... *Birds of a feather flock together.* This goes for people too: rich people typically network with the rich, poor people network with the poor, and the middle class hang out with the middle class. Robert Kiyosaki continues ... "*If you want to become rich, you need to network with those who are rich who can help you become rich.*" And with *I-Commerce* this process starts from the beginning with a formal face-to-face introduction to the business concept by a qualified member of an existing professional business team.

The process continues when the individual joins the team, plugs into a proven system and begins operations. The new member of the team is introduced to leaders who provide direction and mentoring ... leaders who have a vested interest in the success of the new team member.

Although the *I-Commerce* infrastructure is Internet based, it is nonetheless a people-centered business. You can't network with serious success oriented people via computer or with handout brochures or from between the covers of a book. It requires personal interface and interaction. Networking is not an introspective solo effort ... it is a serious social activity that requires teamwork.

Even though the income potential is substantial, don't be misled ... *I-Commerce* is not a get-rich-quick scheme. Everything comes with a price, and the level of income and the degree of wealth attained is directly proportional to desire, competitive spirit and effort. However, in today's changing economy—in today's advancing *Information Age*—there is no better opportunity available for the ambitious individual with a dream!

To find out more about the *I-Commerce* opportunity,
provide the contact information requested at
agreatlifetakesmoney.com

We are all born into the great American adventure ... but only a few choose to strive for greatness!
The doors are open to *I-Commerce* for those with the desire to pass into the future!

BIBLIOGRAPHY

1. Robert Kiyosaki, *Rich Dad's Advisors*
   a. Rich Dad, Poor Dad, What the Rich Teach Their Kids About Money That the Poor and Middle Class Do Not!
   b. CASHFLOW Quadrant, Rich Dad's Guide to Financial Freedom
   c. Rich Dad's Guide to Investing, What the Rich Invest In, That the Poor and Middle Class Do Not!
   d. Retire Young, Retire Rich, How to Get Rich Quickly and Stay Rich Forever
   e. Loop-Holes of the Rich, How the Rich Legally Make More Money & Pay Less Taxes
2. Donald Trump and Robert Kiyosaki
   a. WHY WE WANT YOU TO BE RICH, Two Men, One Message
3. Kevin Phillips
   a. WEALTH AND DEMOCRACY, A Political History of the American Rich
4. Eric D. Beinhocker
   a. *THE ORIGIN OF WEALTH, Evolution, Complexity, and the Radical Remaking of Economics*
5. Pete Engardio
   a. CHINDIA, How China and India Are Revolutionizing Global Business
6. Lawrence Kitlikoff & Scott Burns
   a. THE COMING GENERATIONAL STORM, What You Need to Know About America's Economic Future
7. Stephen R. Covey
   a. The 7 Habits of Highly Effective People
   b. The 8th Habit, From Effectiveness to Greatness

8. James M. Kouzes & Barry Z. Posner
   a. The LEADERSHIP CHALLENGE
9. Stan Davis & Christopher Meyer
   a. BLUR, The Speed of Change in the Connected Economy
10. Joel A. Barker
    a. PARADIGMS, The Business of Discovering the Future
    b. PARADIGMS REGAINED, A Further Exploration of the Mysteries of Modern Science
11. James E. Davidson and Lord William Rees-Mogg
    a. THE SOVEREIGN INDIVIDUAL, Mastering The Transition to the Information Age
12. John C. Maxwell
    a. BECOMING A PERSON OF INFLUENCE, How to Positively Impact the Lives of Others
    b. THINKING FOR A CHANGE, 11 Ways Highly Successful People Approach Life and Work
    c. DEVELOPING THE LEADER WITHIN YOU
    d. DEVELOPING THE LEADERS AROUND YOU, How to Help Others Reach Their Full Potential
13. David McNally
    a. EVEN EAGLES NEED A PUSH, Learning to Soar In a Changing World
14. Alvin Toffler
    a. Future Shock
    b. The Third Wave
    c. Power Shift

978-0-595-50754-2
0-595-50754-9